The Right Way to Live

Plato's Republic
for Catholic Students

2nd Edition

Dr. Richard Geraghty

En Route Books and Media, LLC

St. Louis, MO

Make the time

En Route Books and Media, LLC
5705 Rhodes Avenue
St. Louis, MO 63109

Cover credit: Dr. Sebastian Mahfood, OP

LCCN: 2020953021
ISBN-13: 978-1-952464-48-5

Copyright © 1994, 2021 Richard Geraghty

All rights reserved. No part of this book may be reproduced, stored in a retrieval system, or transmitted in any form, or by any means, without the prior written permission of the publisher.

This book is dedicated to my wife, Rebecca, to Ronda Chervin, and to Peter and Carla Conley.

FOREWORD TO THE 2021 EDITION

Re-released at a time when the world is midway through the coronavirus pandemic, where millions are unemployed, hungry, and homeless, and the United States is facing one of its worst social and political divides in its history, Richard Geraghty's *The Right Way to Live: Plato's Republic for Catholic Students* has something profound to give us, namely an understanding of Socrates' exploration of the nature of justice, which remains as much a concern for us now as it was two and a half millennia ago in Athens, Greece.

The question of whether any virtue is a means to an end, or an end in and of itself, is an important one for us to consider. If a virtue is only a means to an end, then it has use-value that allows for corruption, but if it's an end in and of itself, then it's something to be pursued for its own sake for the purpose of helping us realize the fullness of our lives. That is, we cultivate the virtues because they offer us the right way to live, and we avoid the vices because they offer us nothing but the wrong way to live.

Plato's concern with the moral virtue of justice, then, is no small matter for us today; it is, in fact, a very great matter as we look out onto the social and political landscape of the 2020s, the eve of what might be the end of the world as we know it and the promise of a new beginning as only we can make it.

DR. SEBASTIAN MAHFOOD, OP
JANUARY 3, 2021

FOREWORD TO THE 1994 EDITION

Plato thought philosophy could be exciting, dramatic, ironic, incisive, and profound. Geraghty agrees and proves it in *The Right Way to Live: Plato's Republic for Catholic Students.*

As one introduced to philosophy by Plato, I have never lost my love for his dialogues, yet have never found a way to teach them effectively. I would find myself summarizing Plato's ideas instead of leading students into the dialogue.

Geraghty, a long-term colleague of mine, has found a way to do just this: he takes the student by one hand and Plato by the other and shows how the truths of the old sage are both delightfully and challengingly perennial.

In team-taught philosophy classes, I have seen it work. Plato's *Republic* provides a compelling argument for the absoluteness of morality in an age of skepticism.

In the Catholic battle for moral sanity, we can use such an ally, whose philosophy is made perfectly lucid and available by a master teacher!

RONDA CHERVIN
JULY 25, 1994

TABLE OF CONTENTS

Introduction i
Ch. 1—An Exercise in Objectivity 1
Ch. 2—The Knowledge Supplied by
        Conscience 27
Ch. 3—Popular Morality 49
Ch. 4—Enter the Antagonist 69
Ch. 5—The Basic Question 93
Ch. 6—The View of the Sophist 123
Ch. 7—Socrates Begins His Answer 151
Ch. 8—The Final Definition of Justice as an
        Intrinsic Good 179
Ch. 9—The Portrait of Justice as a Useful
        Good 209
Ch. 10—The Divine Causes 237
Afterword 257
Index 269
About the Author 279

INTRODUCTION

The inspiration for this book, *The Right Way to Live: Plato's Republic for Catholic Students*, 2nd Edition, came after I was presented with the task of teaching philosophical ethics in a Catholic College during the eighties. To teach ethics to college students in any decade is a challenging task. Yet, I realized that this task was nothing compared to the job of teaching moral theology. Ethics is approached from the viewpoint of reason, which everyone is supposed to possess. But moral theology is approached from the viewpoint of Faith, which only Catholics are supposed to possess. And being a real Catholic necessarily involves being obedient to the Magisterium of the Church.

This mixture of ethics, Church, and Magisterium did not go down very well with many of the students or, for that matter, with many of the faculty either. The priests in the theology department, men loyal to the Church, were being bitterly attacked as being pre-Vatican II moralists who were still opposed to pre-marital sex, contraception, divorce, homosexuality, and abortion. They still taught about the existence of heaven and hell. I, myself, was not against the priests, who were simply basing themselves upon what the Church teaches. But I was not exactly for them either. They seemed too grumpy and reactionary and not, I thought, compassionate or pastoral enough.

Today, I have a better idea of why they were so besieged and why I wanted to distance myself from them a bit. After the encyclical *Humanae Vitae* (1968), in which Pope Paul VI condemned contraception,

Introduction

many Catholic intellectuals attacked the truth of this prohibition, thus rejecting the traditional notions of faith and reason. They were rejecting reason because they disagreed with the natural law[1] teaching regarding sexuality in general and contraception in particular. And they were rejecting faith because, in contesting the truth of the teaching, they were implicitly rejecting the authority of the Pope.

There arose in Catholic circles the unCatholic notion that matters that were formerly decided by the Magisterium were now to be decided by the conscience of each believer. Like many other Catholics, I was not aware, at the time, how radical these attacks

---

[1] Central to the intellectual tradition of the Catholic Church is the teaching that there is such a thing as the natural law, which, having been written by God into the very conscience of man, informs humanity with the basic knowledge of right and wrong, independently of any of the teachings of the Old and New Testaments.

were. But I was awash in a certain kind of mood or spirit in which any priest or teacher who held to the teaching of the Pope seemed a bit dogmatic, old-fashioned, rigid, and unsympathetic.

Now, I marvel at my ignorance and timidity as far as Church teaching was concerned. But the fact was that I had always been more interested in philosophy than in theology. I am ashamed to confess it now, but frankly, I thought that theology was quite boring. Moreover, I thought that there were plenty of priests, theologians, Bishops, Cardinals and Popes to ensure that the truth in faith and morals would be preserved.

It was inconceivable to me that there might be modern day heresies and outright revolts within the highest ranks of the Church. It seemed to me that the subject of theology was too boring to generate enough interest to spawn a heresy or revolt. I was a not-very-sterling example of a Catholic professor who was deep in the great tradition of

Introduction

the Church's alliance between faith and reason. I certainly knew about that tradition and, as a student of St. Thomas, even thought that I was an example of it. But, as I have indicated, my grasp of that tradition was more notional than real.

With my imperfect understanding of this tradition, I resolved to teach ethics according to the truth of natural law tradition without acknowledging the role of St. Thomas and of the Church in formulating that tradition. Still, I would deal with ethics as a matter of truths to which I was committed. I would not adopt the approach of many of my fellow professors, who served the ideal that they must be detached or neutral to be intellecttually objective. To me, they seemed to be giving up the idea of being a professor to become managers of an intellectual supermarket whose function was to present enough variety in their products to allow customers the widest freedom of choice.

The book that most readily served my purposes was *The Republic* of Plato. It was a philosophical classic written by a thinker who was also a literary genius. Plato could write, as well as think. And I needed an author who could provoke some interest. As much as I loved Aristotle and St. Thomas, I was not ready to use them in the war zone that was ethics. Moreover, *The Republic* is a seminal work, written at the dawn of Western Civilization. Maybe I could overawe the students a bit-perhaps shame them into some kind of respect for tradition. And even better, it was written by a pagan who happened to be born over four hundred years before Christ. When the students objected, as I was sure they would, at Plato's high moral tone, I could innocently make the rejoinder that it was neither I nor the Church that was talking. It was an old pagan who did not even have the benefit of knowing Revelation when he laid down his teachings. It seemed that I had a

Introduction

perfect shelter if feelings ran too high in the class discussions!

In many respects, *The Republic* would serve as an example of the natural law in action. Even his mistakes (and they are atrocious in the area of sexual ethics, as we will see later) would be instructive.

The great surprise I had at the end of the course was not the effect that the teachings of Plato had upon the students-it was the effect those teachings had upon me. I began to be grateful to the Church and to those faithful priests for holding to its stands on morality. Instead of seeming like cranky old dinosaurs, they now looked like outnumbered defenders of an ancient lighthouse. The Church was that lighthouse, still trying to give direction to a humanity that often despised it. Why this change in view? Plato showed me that the fate of a supremely good man is often to be killed by the powers that be. His hero, Socrates, argues for the existence of moral absolutes, for the nobility of seeking justice for its own sake, for the necessity of objective and unchanging moral norms. Athens, the city he loves, responds to his arguments by executing him.

This portrayal of an ancient Greek reminded me forcefully of Christ, who is a man as supremely good as God because he is God. This God-Man is hung naked on a cross as a result of his effort to save his own people. And the remembrance of Christ recalled to me his Church, which is despised and ridiculed by many as if she were a doddering, old Victorian lady who refuses to let any of her children enjoy life. In short, my teaching of Plato led me to see the Church as the guardian of real liberty and to discover the world as a smooth liar whose advice will lead those following it into slavery, either physical or spiritual, or both.

As I have indicated, Plato's *Republic* is a masterpiece, utilizing all the techniques of a literary master to etch out a picture which will impress itself upon the imagination and

Introduction

heart. But Plato was also a first-rate philosopher, and so has utilized all the techniques of abstract thought to impress the intellect. In my book, I will leave it to Plato to impress the heart of the reader. But as far as his appeal to the intellect is concerned, I will follow his argument as closely and intelligently as I can. For the argument is one of the best ways to initiate a student into the subject of philosophy. And that subject is one of the best ways to initiate a student into a love and grasp of the universal truth about man and morality. There are other and more important ways to attain this truth. For example, those without Revelation must still listen to their consciences and pray to God. Catholics must listen to the Church and pray to the Trinity and honor Mary. To be religious, one does not have to be a philosopher.

Yet, the Church has always encouraged those who have the opportunity for a higher education to develop their reason through the study of philosophy. The human intellect is a great power. If it is not kept under the control of a pure heart, it will destroy the conscience of a culture by making moral sensitivity look repressive and narrow. Reason will then paint a picture of a free, intelligent, and sun-filled future in which man's true potential will be realized.

Reason, under the control of the Sophists, did this in old Athens. And reason, under the control of modern influences, has done this in the present day. Just as Plato did not abandon the use of reason to the Sophists, so the Church has never abandoned the use of reason to the enemies of the Faith. The Church has always known that if reason does not learn how to be humble in regard to the Church, in the way that a creaturely gift must bow to a divine one, it will oppose the faith of the Church as a deadly enemy. It behooves me, therefore, to give the best introduction to philosophy that I know how to give. In thus rehabilitating Reason, I will be helping Faith.

Introduction

And so I write this book as a help to the students' understanding of *The Republic* of Plato so that they might become alive to the great Catholic tradition of faith and reason.

CHAPTER ONE

AN EXERCISE IN OBJECTIVITY

INTRODUCTION

One of the great difficulties of the Church today is that modern culture seems to accept without any doubts or reservations a morality that is relativistic. Consequently, the culture takes as the normal state of affairs that there be a wide variety of views on such matters as abortion, contraception, divorce, pre-marital sex, adultery, homosexuality, euthanasia, and suicide. On matters of religious opinion, which usually involve views about morality, the culture also seems to show the same tolerance for diversity. The only time it seems to lose its cool, so to speak, is when the Church proclaims itself as the One True Church and labels all of the actions above as intrinsically evil, not only upon the basis of faith, but also upon the basis of reason. Then the culture, relativistic on every other issue, is absolutistic on this one; namely, that the Church is wrong, close-minded, judgmental, intolerant, authoritarian, tyrannical, repressed, and irrational.

Why is the culture so sure that it is right? To most people the answer is clear. They think it highly improbable that, of all the different religions and churches in the world, there can be such a thing as The One True Church. Anyone even entertaining the possibility of such a notion is in their eyes a person of extraordinary arrogance and close-mindedness. They also think that the odds against this Church being right in its many judgments about intrinsic evils are astronomical, especially when that claim is sup-

Ch. 1 An Exercise in Objectivity

posed to be based upon reason. Since people feel that their powers of reason are at least as good as anyone else's, they are especially provoked by the claim that the natural law teaching is the only one based upon reason. In the minds of many people today, the case is that simple moral relativism is obviously reasonable while moral absolutism is just as obviously unreasonable.

Since a culture sets the intellectual milieu in which our mind breathes, so to speak, we Catholics must take special steps that the modern bias does not lead us to abandon the use of reason in discussing morality. Or, to put the matter less benignly, since our culture is becoming increasingly outraged and antagonistic to the stand of the Church (reminding me of the ancient Roman charge that the Church is the enemy of the people), we Catholics must not be frightened out of trying to think about and understand our natural law heritage.

One way to grasp that point for ourselves is to study *The Republic* of Plato, which is especially adept at sorting out the reality from the appearance, the truth from the lie, and the light from the shadow. But we will need a preparation for this task that appeals to both our imagination and our intellect.

To heal our imaginations, we will in the first part consider the problem of building a house in the right way. Yes! I said building a house. I could just as well have said fixing a toilet, building a boat, or training a dog. The point is that when it comes to technical answers, we Americans are quite objective, precise, and hardheaded. If our toilet overflows after the plumber supposedly fixed it, no one is going to convince us that the plumber is a good one or a bad one depending on how one looks at the matter. In matters of morality, someone may be able to talk to us in that manner. But in matters of plumbing no one can tell us that the worker is not objectively, absolutely, realistically, and

Ch. 1 An Exercise in Objectivity

literally incompetent. In other words, a lousy plumber. It will do our imaginations good, then, to recall that in some matters of life, we can be quite sure that there is a right and a wrong way to do something. Then, we might be more ready to consider the matter of the right way to live.

The second thing we will do in this chapter will be to heal our intellects. We will discuss the technical arts again, only this time from the angle of the formal process of definition. Now this process is a rather humble and pedestrian affair, particularly as it was used by Socrates. He was always mixing up his definitions of justice, virtue, and goodness with definitions of ship builders, carpenters, and shepherds. For the process of definition is the ideal instrument for pushing people to think again after they have been swimming around in the fog of relativism for a long time. In relativism, nothing is what it is; things exist only as they appear to others. A murderer can be a sadist, a revolutionary, a hero, or a victim all depending on the different views one can take of him. In defining things, however, we mark them off, draw limits or boundaries around them, make them clear. We say what the thing is in itself, irrespective of the almost infinite number of views that one can take of it. The definition of a car or a house will tell us exactly what a house is in itself as opposed to the way it may appear to others. The definition of justice or virtue will also tell us what those entities really are and not what they appear to be. It is no mystery, then, why Plato has designed the whole Republic as a long search for the definition of justice. He is trying to locate the edges of the truth again after they had been blurred by many controversies.

THE RIGHT WAY TO BUILD A HOUSE

Let us suppose that we are trying to set up an intellectual inquiry into the right way to

Ch. 1 An Exercise in Objectivity

build a house. I say an *intellectual* inquiry because, if we were trying to be practical, we wouldn't bother with this inquiry at all. Instead, we would contact some builders whom we trusted and get on with getting our house built. Here, however, our interest is more academic.

First, we go abroad and collect people who have various perspectives on the matter. Of course, we include a good number of actual house builders. We also include real estate people and psychologists. They all have some experience and interest in houses for the family. (Since we intend to find the right way, we don't want to miss any truth that experts in these particular fields might bring us.)

THE EXPERIENCED CARPENTERS

Let us make ourselves the chair of this group with, therefore, the prerogative of setting the question. We announce that the topic is whether there is such a thing as the right way to build a house. We then give the floor to a grizzled old builder. He mutters a few words, which no one understands. He is a builder, not a public speaker. Moreover, he resents the presence of all the other parties, thinking that the topic only belongs to builders like himself. He is not very eager to participate in what he thinks is an idiotic project.

We graciously let the man sit down, but inwardly we are disappointed. While the carpenters probably know more about the matter than anybody else does, they are not interested in discussing it.

REAL ESTATE BROKERS

So, we now move on to the real estate representatives, who certainly have experience in speaking! The real estate people say that the right way to build a house is to create a building that meets the needs of the family.

Ch. 1 An Exercise in Objectivity

They point out that while wigwams, igloos, straw huts, house boats, mobile homes and even caves have been used to meet some family's needs, they are not houses in the way that Americans use the term. Their point is well taken because it adds some precision to the group's use of the term *house*.

The realtors go on to point out that while good builders are an essential factor in producing such a product, they are not the only ones. Many a good product, they point out, has bankrupted its producer because he did not package it properly. Hence, one must include in the definition of the right way to build not only the builder, but the real estate person as well.

We, perhaps having been stung in the past by a slick operator, ask whether it is possible that there is a conflict between building a good house and selling it. We would have thought that building it was one skill and selling it was an entirely another skill. The real estate people get a bit nervous at this question, knowing how often the resources that should go into making a product are shifted to packaging it. They have seen how customers, not knowing much, often prefer the appearance they can see to the realities they cannot see.

They answer that while in theory, the *rightness* of the house has nothing to do with packaging and everything to do with the building of it, in practice both are tied together. Therefore, they maintain, it is proper to include the notion of packaging with the notion of the right way to build.

THE ECONOMISTS

We feel inclined to question this view, but, in the interest of politeness and of getting on with the project, we instead move on to inquire of the economists. They maintain that the right way to build a house is determined by the market. What is in demand is built the right way. What is not in demand is built the wrong way.

We demur from such a stand, saying that surely one cannot make the laws of supply and demand the basic standard of judging the right way to build a house. At this point, the economists look at us pityingly: to them, we are starry-eyed idealists, still pushing for the old-fashioned idea that a carpenter can build a good house even if no one buys it. They follow up their condescending looks with a speech that distracts the audience from their cynical approach by mocking our innocence. Everybody gets a good laugh at how naive we intellectuals are.

THE DIFFICULTY

Let us sit back a moment now and reflect on the experience recounted above. The first thing that strikes us is that even a relatively simple matter such as discovering the right way to build a house is not so simple. In fact, if we increase the worth of the house by a thousand-fold and bring in more experts and consultants, we may be tempted to utter despair. Assuming we can control our pride, sweet reason will prevail. When people do not let their pride, greed, and competitiveness override their reason they handle simple projects with ease and more complicated ones with some difficulty. But they handle them. However, this is not often the case. What is the one great feature that reason shows us in its effort to teach us the great lesson about objectivity? It is the all-importance of the *purpose* of any human activity.

THE GOAL

Amid all the confusion that ensues when we attend to the question of the right way to build a house, we have to see that there must be some purpose or goal in building it. If it has no goal or purpose, it will not exist and

Ch. 1 An Exercise in Objectivity

neither will the other factors that follow as a consequence of its existence.

This point is obvious enough. But let's push it one step further. The purpose of any house determines how it will be built. And how it will be built will determine how the carpenter will act. That, in turn, will determine the type of skills and knowledge he will need to acquire to become good at his work. Finally, the purpose of any house will determine whether an actual house is any good or not. For example, if the purpose of a house is to shelter people, a house with a great hole in the roof will not be a good one. Nor will the builder of such a house be a good builder.

To put the matter succinctly: the purpose of any human activity is the reason that activity is done. It is also the reason the activity has the nature it has. And it is the objective standard by which this activity and its agent are considered good or bad. If one wishes to cross the sea, then one will have to engage in the activity of building a ship. This ship and the carpenter producing it will be good if the ship enables one to cross the sea. If it sinks as soon as it is launched, the ship and everything connected with its production are all bad.

Here we have the objective heart of the matter when discussing the worth of any human activity, including, of course, the activity of leading a human life. One has to take the goal of that activity and then judge whether that goal is reached. If it is reached, the activity and its agent are good. If it is not reached; the activity and its agent are bad. That, in a nutshell, is what this whole book is about.

By this point, we have at least partially achieved our purpose of healing our imaginations by recalling that there is, at least, objectivity in technical matters. We have also put our finger upon the reason why objectivity is possible, thus beginning an intellectual cure for the relativism abounding in our milieu. Now, let us proceed to sharpen our ideas even more by considering the process of definition.

THE PROCESS OF DEFINITION

To define a house is to answer the question of what it is. To answer this question, one cannot simply point to a particular house. Many can point out a house from among other types of buildings. But far fewer can describe a house in such a way that this description will fit houses and only houses. To speak technically, to be able to point out a house is to have ordinary experience of the thing to be defined. In other words, one has sense experience of the particular thing in question. However, to be able to define a house is to know its nature or essence. Here, one can demonstrate intellectual or rational knowledge of the particular thing in question.

A COMMON PROCESS

There is nothing particularly abstruse about the process of proceeding from sense experience to rational knowledge of any particular house. The first step of the process is the experience that one must have of many particular houses. It is obvious why this first step is necessary—one can't determine what houses have in common until one has seen some houses.

The second step is to discover a universal term, which will include within its field, all the particulars in question. For example, we might call a house a building. In logic, this act of placing the thing to be defined in a general classification is called placing it in a genus. The merit of generic placement is that it includes houses while excluding caves, motor homes, and houseboats. This is what definition does—it marks off one class from another.

Ch. 1 An Exercise in Objectivity

The third step is to differentiate the house from all the other things that may be found in the generic category of building. If we picture the category of *building* as a huge circle including houses, jails, dormitories, skyscrapers, churches, hotels, and stadiums, we would have to find a term that would fit houses and only houses. That term would differentiate houses from all the other buildings and so is called a *differentia* in logic.

How would we find the term that would differentiate houses from all the other entities in the genus of building? We would employ what is called the *counterexample*. Let us say that a person tries to differentiate a house from other buildings by calling it a place where people live. Another person would immediately point out that people live in jails and hotels. Hence, the differentia does not really differentiate a house from all the other buildings. To call a house a building in which people live is too broad a definition.

The last step in the process will be to qualify the notion of a building such that the result will fit houses and only houses and nothing but houses. Let us say, then, that a house is a building designed to provide shelter for from one to two families. Perhaps that definition is not yet perfect, but it will suffice for our purposes.

We have now grasped the nature or essence of *house*, *what* any house is, in itself, independently of how anyone might look at it. This is a limited, finite, definite thing though the views one may take of it are unlimited, infinite, and indefinite. With this definition in mind, we are ready to deal with any meeting on the right way to build a house.

PHILOSOPHICAL ANALYSIS

The example above indicates a general truth about all definitions of man-made entities. It is impossible to define them without stating their purpose. In determining that the purpose for the design of a house is to provide shelter for a family, one has marked a house off from absolutely all the other entities in the genus of building. Similarly, one cannot know what a car or a boat or a gun is unless one knows what it is for. The same goes for the technical arts. One cannot define the art of doctoring without including the goal of healing people or the art of teaching without including the goal of imparting the truth. Understanding the goal or purpose of an art is the key to making the art, its activity, and its practitioners intelligible.

REPEATING THE POINT

To summarize what we've learned; we see that defining the goal of any art automatically supplies one with the standard by which to judge the right from the wrong way of performing it. This definition of the goal cannot be arbitrary. It is not an arbitrary matter that a doctor heals, a teacher teaches, an orator gives speeches, and a policeman keeps the peace. The definition does not depend upon how the definer wishes to look at the matter. One may have his theories about all the above. But a definer is not producing a pet theory. If he is giving a true definition, he is necessarily objective and the definition is absolute, meaning that it is what it is and is not anything else. In the light of this standard, all other things relating to an activity are judged.

DEFINITION AND THE RIGHT WAY TO LIVE

Let us now apply the lessons we have learned about definition to the matter of the right way to live. The purpose of *The Republic* is to answer the question "What is

Ch. 1 An Exercise in Objectivity

justice?"[2] This question is another way to ask what the right way to live is, for if we ask what justice is, we are asking what is the just or good thing to do. And doing what is just or good is the same as living the right way.

We have seen that the process of definition must start from a foundation in which the particular things to be defined are known through ordinary experience. What is that ordinary experience in the case of virtue? What are the particular acts one calls virtuous, which, if analyzed, will lead to the definition of virtue?

Here, of course, we are not speaking of a product like a house. We are speaking of a

---

[2] The word "justice" is an English translation of a Greek word, which has a much wider meaning than its English rendition. For Plato, justice means the same thing as goodness or virtue. It includes both the moral and the legal. It designates the one quality that both the individual and the community need to live correctly.

human action that is considered to be good. People may not be used to thinking of actions as particular realities. But they are real things that make a real difference. Ask anyone at the receiving end of a gift—or a punch! The difference is that actions do not exist on their own like houses; they depend for their existence upon the agents who perform them.

To return to the question: what are the actions whose goodness is so obvious that they will constitute the facts, which will lead to a definition of virtue? Some such actions are to tell the truth, to pay back debts, and to honor one's parents. On the opposite side of the questions lie actions such as murder, rape, and pillage. Here, the basic contention is that human beings have, by the fact that they are human, the knowledge that certain actions are right and others are wrong. One may call this knowledge *natural* to any human being who has the use of reason. One can also call this knowledge experiential because it is not a theoretical view about the

Ch. 1 An Exercise in Objectivity

nature of good or evil. Rather it is the judgment in particular cases. One can judge that murder is wrong in a particular case without being able to define the terms *murder* or *wrong*, just as one is able to say that a house with a leaky roof is a bad one without being able to defend that judgment against a real estate lawyer for the other side.

One does not need much experience to know that a house without a roof on it is a poor one or that a ship with a huge hole in its bottom is terribly inadequate. Of course, one does need some notion of what a house or a ship is to make even these judgments. So, too, one does not have to know much about mothers to know that their children should not beat or torment them or much about children to know that they should not be sexually abused.[3] One with just the ordinary experience of life would know these things.

---

[3] Here, we're not discussing the actions of the criminally insane, or those who hear God's voice asking them to commit murder.

Of course, to claim that human beings have a natural knowledge of right and wrong is not to claim that they will necessarily follow it. A knowledge that is natural to man does not take away his freedom of choice. People who know it is wrong to murder can still choose to murder someone. So, too, a carpenter who knows that a house should have a roof is not thereby compelled to put a roof on a particular house he is building.

ANOTHER TYPE OF EXPERIENCE

There is another type of experiential knowledge, however, that is not natural but acquired. When people choose to live by their natural knowledge, they begin to form habits, which solidify their character in goodness. They become more clear-sighted and more effective in determining and following the right way to act in the many and difficult circumstances of life. Of course, a person may choose to disregard his natural knowledge in

Ch. 1 An Exercise in Objectivity

electing to lead a life of preying upon his fellow man. This person, too, will develop habits that will solidify his character but solidify it in vice. He will be alert to spot his main chance; his conscience will be hardened enough not to bother him about any crime he may have to perpetrate in order to attain his ends.

Thus, we see that the way a person chooses to live will hone and define his ability to understand and practice the objective values inherent in natural knowledge.

The analogue for this type of moral experience in the field of the technical arts is the type that a skilled carpenter acquires in the course of pursuing his trade. Any fool can know that a house without a roof or ships without a bottom are poor products. And any klutz has enough ability to take a hammer and nail some boards to build some kind of rough shelter. But only a skilled carpenter can judge the fine points of a house or do the work required to produce one.

LOOKING AHEAD

We have tried to heal our imaginations by considering that, at least in the technical arts, we hold that reason and objectivity have a place. We have also tried to tune up our intellects by analyzing the process of definition, whose purpose is to clarify what things are in themselves, not simply how they appear to others. We are now ready to begin our analysis of *The Republic*.

CHAPTER 2

TO KNOWLEDGE SUPPLIED BY CONSCIENCE

INTRODUCTION

In this chapter, we will analyze the very first part of Book One of *The Republic* in order to observe how Plato lays down the foundation of his inquiry into the nature of justice. This is the most critical part of the whole process of definition because it supplies the material out of which the definition will be fashioned. If the right material is not present in the foundations, the definition cannot be right. We saw this point verified in our analysis of the definition of a house. For one to reach the right definition of a house, one has to start with the experience of particular entities that are indeed houses. That there are particular entities called houses is the fact upon which all the inquirers must be in agreement. The point upon which they need not agree is the nature or essence of house itself. This, they will have to delve into by comparing their general formulations with the facts themselves.

The same holds true for success in defining the nature of justice or virtue. To get the right definition, the inquirers must agree with each other about the identity of individual actions as just or virtuous. They must, for example, take for granted that it is right for children to obey their parents and that it is wrong for parents to abuse their child sexually. After agreeing that certain kinds of actions are right and others are wrong, the inquirers are ready to search for the nature itself of rightness or wrongness.

Ch. 2 To Knowledge Supplied by Conscience

People cannot very well search for the nature of justice before they agree that just deeds exist.

Right away, the reader can see that it will be a far more difficult matter for Plato to establish the foundations for his inquiry into the nature of justice than it was for us to establish the foundations for an inquiry into the nature of a house. Yet the general outline of the task is the same since both tasks are examples of the same process, that of definition.

Before proceeding to an analysis of Book One to see how Plato sets his foundations, let us try to show how he is especially suited to his task because of his large experience of life. Since the outcome of an inquiry into the right way to live can be only as good as the experience from which it is drawn, we should take some pains to establish the credentials of Plato in this matter.

PLATO THE AUTHOR

What kind of person is the author? He was born into a noble family prominent in the affairs of Athens. Thus, in experiencing the normal interplay between family members, he also experienced the political life of the city. A Kennedy or a Rockefeller might be a modern example of such an upbringing. Through their family, relatives, and friends they are in contact not only with current affairs of political significance but with the past as well. They do not have to study history merely from books. They have but to listen to the stories of grandparents, uncles, and aunts.

The prominence of Plato's family made him a natural for some type of political leadership. Athens needed good leadership. Having become, along with Sparta, the liberators of the Greek world from the power of the Persians, Athens was later engaged in a war with Sparta for supremacy in that world.

Ch. 2 To Knowledge Supplied by Conscience

This war between democratic and commercial Athens with aristocratic and militaristic Sparta not only divided the other city-states but also the citizens within each state. Thus, Athens was undergoing the strain, not only of fighting for survival with outsiders, but of trying to moderate the hostility between the democratic and aristocratic factions within its own walls. Yet Plato did not follow his family destiny. Instead of becoming a politician, he became a political philosopher.

THE INFLUENCE OF SOCRATES

Like many other young men of his generation, Plato was disillusioned with the chaos of the times and took an interest in the inquiries conducted by Socrates with many of the powerful figures in Athens. At the age of twenty-eight, however, he was shocked to see Socrates condemned to death by many of the same figures. A few years earlier, he had experienced the fall of the city, which was never again to resume its former greatness.

The young Plato resolved not to fallow the role laid out for him by his family because he was disgusted with the dishonesty shown by all sides of the political spectrum, even his own relatives. Instead, he continued the mission of Socrates in trying to wake Athens into awareness that it had a soul. Unlike his mentor, who never wrote anything, Plato composed masterpieces, thus earning for himself the honor of being, among other things, the founder of political philosophy.

When Plato wrote *The Republic* around 380 BC, he was a middle-aged man who had already had twenty years to reflect upon the fall of Athens and the death of his mentor. During those years, he engaged in several ventures which put him at the heart of the political power in Syracuse. He was lucky to escape with his life and found that trying to teach philosophy to future rulers could be a very dangerous enterprise.

Ch. 2 To Knowledge Supplied by Conscience

In summary, Plato is one of the few great philosophers in the Western Tradition who was intimately acquainted with those who exercised political power. Professors usually meet these figures only in books or in managed interviews. Plato knew them in person.

THE LITERARY FORM

The literary form of the book makes it particularly apt for dealing with wide experience in life. It is a dramatic dialogue in which Plato speaks, never in his own name, but through the characters he has created. Thus, the book could be put directly on stage without any changes in the script. The characters in the play, however, are not mere creations of Plato. They are real people from history. Thus, their opinions are the kinds of opinions real people express.

The whole book is a word-by-word account given by Socrates of a conversation he had in the past with a group of friends. The conversation is an inquiry into the meaning of justice, about which the group widely differs. Thus, the literary creation of Plato draws its inspiration from real life figures, which are concerned with morality from the viewpoint not only of individuals but also of the whole community. This form, then, is an ideal vehicle, not just for showing various philosophical views, but also the types of characters that espouse these views. This means that the reader is treated to a masterful exposition of abstract thought in a real-life setting. Philosophers speak abstractly, novelists speak concretely, and Plato speaks Plato.

THE CHARACTERS IN THE DRAMA

Let us now took at the cast of characters that Plato introduces to us in Book One of his work. Through the voice of Socrates, Plato presents four speaking characters. They congregate in a house beyond the city for a favorite pastime, a good debate. Scholars conjecture that the setting for the discussion is around 424 BC, over twenty years before the fall of Athens to Sparta. The characters in the discussion make no explicit mention of this war, but we may assume it formed a kind of subliminal background to the discussion.

The experience of the characters embraces most of the fifth century of classical Greece.

THE OLDMAN

The old man, Cephalus, though not actually a citizen of Athens, is quite familiar with its affairs. His boyhood and youth were molded by the heady atmosphere in which Athens, allied with Sparta, defeated the Persians, an event that we still commemorate today in our running of the marathon.⁴ This period propelled Athens to the role of being the leader of freedom loving peoples who had repulsed the foreign despot. Greeks considered the men of this generation somewhat in the manner we Americans consider our founding Fathers—as men of heroic stature who set the national type for courage and dedication to the nation.

SOCRATES

Next in age is Socrates, who had already served in an earlier campaign of the Athenians, not against foreigners like the Persians, but against fellow Greeks like the Spartans. Socrates was deeply involved in the life of his city, but never as a public official. He once said that if he had attained public office, he would have been tried for execution

---

⁴ The city of Marathon was the location from whence a man ran twenty miles to Athens to convey the news of the victory over Persia.

Ch. 2 To Knowledge Supplied by Conscience

far sooner than he was. His involvement consisted in carrying on the ordinary duties of a citizen and, more especially, in initiating inquiries.

As we will see later in more detail, his favorite approach was to question people who were supposed to know something about the nature of some virtue or other. Full of their own importance, they would answer with confidence. Socrates would examine their reply by asking another question. After a while, the respondent would start sweating, as his ignorance became apparent, not only to himself, but also to the eagerly listening bystanders. It takes little historical imagination to realize why Socrates was finally executed! To lead others, particularly those who are politically powerful, to a realization that they are really ignorant of the most important political questions is a job with a very low life expectancy!

SOCRATES AND THE OLD MAN[5]

Let us now proceed to first scene. Socrates encounters Cephalus, the old man, seated upon a cushion in his home and wearing a garland after having sacrificed to the gods. The whole party draws up seats around him. Having been warmly greeted, Socrates remarks that he considers conversations with very old people to be among his greatest pleasures. Why? Because the elderly are travelers on a road that the younger have not yet taken but will eventually take. The old man is a veteran of life who has already experienced and made some decisions on how to handle such basic issues as sexuality, money, religion, physical weakness, and the prospect of death.

From the conversation that ensues between Socrates and Cephalus, we learn that the old man does not have the dread of aging

---

[5] See section 328c.

Ch. 2 To Knowledge Supplied by Conscience

that most of his contemporaries have. He claims that the resources of a good character enable him to sustain the burdens of age, burdens that sour the disposition of his peers. He is not being eaten up by griping about his loss of power, both sexual and physical, or about the way he is being treated by the young.

Favorably impressed with these views, Socrates draws him out further. He notes that others will attribute the attitude of the old man to his possession of wealth. The old man answers that, while old age would still be difficult for a virtuous poor man, it will always be a burden to an unvirtuous rich man. In short, he reiterates his opinion that a good character is the most important possession of a human being.

The old man goes on to say that he is presently concerned with the question of death. The teachings of religion come back to haunt him at night with thoughts of the afterlife. Hence the old man uses his considerable wealth to rectify possible misdeeds in the past with regard both to his neighbors and to the gods.

Most of the discussion between the old man and Socrates is in the conversational form of a younger man asking respectfully about the older man's views of life in general. Towards the end of the discussion, however, Socrates takes an abrupt turn. He shifts his questions to a philosophical plane. He asks, 'What is justice?' Here is the typical intellectual challenge of the old philosopher, which invites a group to become inquirers or searchers for a definition.

The old man, knowing that this quest is beyond both his interest and ability, laughingly bequeaths the project to his son. Cephalus leaves the gathering to offer further sacrifices to the gods.

Ch. 2 To Knowledge Supplied by Conscience

A MODERN CONCLUSION

What can we conclude from the fact that Plato opens up his book depicting the process of defining the nature of justice by depicting the views of a religious old man about what a good life is? Furthermore, what can Plato mean when he opens up his book about a philosophical inquiry with an old man who has no interest in philosophy? And what can Plato be saying to us when he portrays Socrates, who certainly is a philosopher, as approving the views of Cephalus?

A thinker with a modern mentality might say that Plato is showing us the superstitious nonsense that a person may fall into if they do not take up the study of philosophy. Since modern thinkers have little or no respect for the moral influence that religion wields, they figure that a genius like Plato has the same lack of respect. Based on this view, Cephalus is a typical instance of the effect that religion has upon people, particularly the old. It wakes them up at three in the morning with guilty thoughts that propel them to make themselves right with others and with God before they die. Since such a picture of a religious person clashes with their view of a fully mature human being, modern thinkers despise this religious type.

They consider the old man to be bound in blind superstition and greatly in need of conducting an inquiry in the nature of justice. They reject any talk about conscience, natural law, God, religion. Modern people are the product of over three hundred years of an intellectual attack upon Christianity, which has penetrated into the mass culture of today. For most of history, atheism was the position of relatively few intellectuals. Today, it is the driving force behind communism and other movements of whole peoples. It is the driving force behind the secularism that is so rife in the United States today.

The modern view is that the philosopher, to be considered objective, must approach all moral questions with the open-mindedness of a scientist observing, for example, the sex life of a fruit fly. In this modern tradition, the philosopher is supposed to 'think' his way to the right position by carefully weighing answers as if he were some kind of balance scale, starting out with no inclinations one way or the other but resting squarely upon zero. These are the assumptions that a modern thinker might hold as legitimate for those setting up an inquiry into the nature of justice or virtue.

THE VIEW OF PLATO

But is that the view of Plato? The answer is no, as we will see more clearly as we get into his book. For now, let me propose another possible explanation of Plates view of the old man. He sees the old man as a noble result of the influence of religion upon human nature, an influence that is not necessarily accompanied by any philosophical training. Here,

Plato takes the same view as all natural law thinkers throughout the ages have taken. They consider that God has implanted in the mind and heart of man a conscience by which he knows naturally that there is a right and a wrong and that he will be judged by God, both in this and the next life for those actions. Furthermore, natural law thinkers hold that those following their consciences become so habituated that they have a keen sense in judging goodness and a strong will in pursuing it. This is what Plato takes to be the experience of a good person in this life.

Based on this view of the matter, all inquirers into the nature of justice or virtue must have the same type of experience of life if they are to agree in their judgment about the justice or injustice of particular deeds. It will not be enough for the inquirers to agree that, for example, it is wrong for an adult to murder someone or to abuse a child. Practically anyone, even those who do these deeds, will agree that they are wrong. No. The

Ch. 2 To Knowledge Supplied by Conscience

inquirers will have to take more or less the same view that Cephalus takes of such things as money, sex, and worship. The old man did not agree about these points with many of his old companions. His seemed to be a minority view against the views of the others. The conclusion is that inquirers who have the proper credentials for their task will already have to be men of solid character.

This view of Plato casts a clear light on the distinction between the practical activity called living a good life and the theoretical activity of defining the nature of a good life. One *lives* a good life by following the basic principles of the natural law so that eventually a solid character is formed which makes the person more expert in doing and judging what is just. On the other hand, one *defines* a good life first by reflecting upon the details that one knows by experience and then defining that experience. Here, it is not the definition of justice that precedes the living of it. Rather it is the other way around. One lives it before one can define it.

It is important for Plato to lay down this point. Otherwise, one might get the impression that before one really knows what virtue or justice is, one must be able to define it. This business of making the discovery of the nature of justice a purely intellectual affair is in fact one of the fallacies of the type of intellect that corrupts a sound religious tradition, destroys the conscience of a culture, and creates the fog of moral relativism. For an intellect not filled with experience is an empty and dangerous thing. If it is not fed by the experience that living by one's conscience provides, then it is fed by the experience of one who does not follow their conscience. With the latter experience, one will not accept the old man as an example of a good person. Instead, one will brand the practices of religion as being entirely superstitious, limited, and narrow. One will set up

Ch. 2 To Knowledge Supplied by Conscience

an entirely new morality to supplant the old one.

In starting out with the portrait of Socrates approving the life experience of the old man, Plato is supplying us with the touchstone of what moral goodness looks like in the real order. In other words, Plato is laying this experience down as the only type of experience which is capable of being the foundation from which a legitimate inquiry into the nature of justice can be launched.

But are these very sane assumptions? When it comes to building a house, do we place the same confidence in an inexperienced builder as we do in an old veteran? Furthermore, is it really sensible for a thinker to be detached or neutral about, for example, eating human beings or sexually abusing children? Is there not something monstrous about taking such a stand? And still further, is it right to make the question about objective morality hinge around many intellecttual considerations rather than hinging around a person being brought up correctly, being introduced to making proper choices? Is it saner to make instruction in morality consist of a lecture appealing to the intellect; or should it consist of being led by a father or mother or elder sibling into the mysteries of how to live a good life?

CHAPTER 3

POPULAR MORALITY

INTRODUCTION

In this chapter, we will examine how Plato introduces us for the first time to a particular use of philosophy. That use is not to create a moral person simply by means of argument. If one is not very moral before starting the study of philosophy, that study will ordinarily make one even less moral because the critical mind that one acquires may lead one to tear apart traditional notions of morality. A great teacher with a soul can use philosophy as a means of waking up or shocking a person who is morally asleep. Socrates will, by his questioning of Polemarchus, the son of the old man, reveal to the young man that he is not as virtuous as he thought he was and that indeed he is in need of moral guidance. In other words, Plato will show us that if we wish to inquire into the nature of justice, we might have to develop a little caution and humility, reexamining our lives and characters before we are ready to undertake that project.

POLEMARCHUS

The young man is of the generation in which Athens is no longer the small power that saved the Greeks from the Persians. Athens is becoming a world power, dominating not only foreigners but also other Greek cities with its commercial and military might. This generation may look back with respect to its founding fathers, the heroes of Marathon, for their simple, manly virtues.

Ch. 3 Popular Morality

But it has also learned how to survive in the struggles in which world powers engage to retain what they consider to be their rightful places. Furthermore, religion does not seem to be honored by this generation as it was by the previous one.

What type of character does Polemarchus have? He seems to be halfway between the past and the future of Athens. He still has ties to the past. He honors the poets and the traditional moral teachers. He abides more or less by conventional morality. He is a decent enough person. Thus, he is something like his father. But he is also something like a man of the new politics. Consequently, he also has something in common with the young radicals, who will be represented by Thrasymachus, whom we will discuss in the next chapter.

GIVE TO EACH WHAT IS OWED HIM

As I mentioned in the last chapter, Socrates announces the main topic of the whole Republic by asking 'What is justice?' As we saw, the old man does not attempt to answer the question of Socrates. He laughingly bequeaths the project to his son. The son confidently puts forth an answer. He starts by quoting, with general approval, a Greek poet and, after being questioned, settles upon the definition that justice is giving each what is owed him.[6] Giving a counterexample, Socrates notes that returning the loan of a weapon to an owner who had gone mad would be an unjust act. Therefore, one cannot define justice, as giving each what is owed him.

---

[6] See section 331E.

Ch. 3 Popular Morality

AN ANALYSIS

Let us analyze this brief exchange for what it reveals to us about the process of definition. There is no disagreement between the two men about the moral facts of the case. They agree that it is just to give another what is due. They also agree that it is unjust to return a sword to an owner who has gone mad. What they disagree about is the definition of the nature of justice. Polemarchus has declared that it is the very nature of justice to give everyone his due. When Socrates proposes the counter-example of the owner gone mad, Polemarchus is confused. A person more adept in thinking might not have been so confused. He might have answered that in the case of the mad man, what was due him was not to return his sword. His definition would have withstood the counterexample of Socrates. But Plato's point is that the young man is not that adept in thinking. He is an example of those people who, because they are so sure that stealing is wrong, are just as sure that they know the definition of stealing.

THE DIFFICULTY UNDERESTIMATED

In this first exchange, we see that the young man has underestimated the difficulty of the question, as might anyone who has not thought much about the matter. He thinks that the question can be easily solved by simply quoting some poet and then using his common sense. Socrates, using a common sense that has been sharpened by years of intellectual training, simply asks a few pertinent questions which prompt the younger man to revise his former definition. Here, Polemarchus is not attacked by another inquirer throwing a long speech at him. Rather he is stunned by the counterexample of Socrates into discovering his own mistakes. That is the purpose of any good communal inquiry—to allow its members to

Ch. 3 Popular Morality

aid each other in the apprehension of the truth.

The mistake of Polemarchus so far has been intellectual, not moral. The fact that he is not intellectually sophisticated does not in itself mean that he is not a good person. (If being moral were the same as being intellectual, then only college students would be moral, with the professors leading the pack!)

But now the discussion takes a turn in which Polemarchus reveals his own character, his own experience of life. Socrates does not counter with his own views and experience. Instead, he continues to ask questions. But his questions have a point which begin to make Polemarchus sense that there are contradictions in his own position. We will select one example from the subsequent exchange to show that ultimately it is not differences in intellectual ability, but differences in the experience of life that separate the younger man from Socrates in a way that Cephalus, the old father, is not separated.

JUSTICE AS THE ART OF DOING GOOD TO FRIENDS AND HARM TO ENEMIES[7]

After having received some hints from Socrates on how to define things, Polemarchus finally declares justice to be an art in which one does good to friends and harm to enemies. Socrates, behaving more like a fellow inquirer than an opponent, accepts this definition provisionally in order to examine it more carefully.

The reason he is a fellow inquirer is that, for the moment, he shares a common ground with the young man. In looking at all the instances of justice that he can think of, Socrates is willing to grant that justice is some kind of an art. In other words, "art" is the

---

[7] See section 332d.

Ch. 3 Popular Morality

generic term, the first universal notion, under which all instances of justice or virtue are placed. Why is Socrates willing to share this view with the young man?

The answer consists in the way in which the Greeks view an art. It is the acquired ability to perform a deed well. Any person possessing an art, then, is considered especially capable of acting well. Thus, there is a similarity between a just person and a skilled artisan. Of course, the Greeks also acknowledge the basic difference between good craftsmen and good persons. No more than we, would they hold that a great builder or athlete or doctor is necessarily a good human being. Like us, they might be tempted to make such an equation. Yet they also had enough experience in life to recognize that a great "Father of the People" may beat his wife and desert his children. Great public figures may be vicious private monsters. There is enough in Greek experience, then, to alert them to the danger of identifying too closely the art of living with the other arts.

At any rate, both Socrates and Polemarchus agree to consider justice as some kind of an art. The task is now to identify the particular kind of art that justice is. Under the terms of logic, they must discover the characteristic that differentiates the art of justice from all the other arts. This differentiation comes from distinguishing the goal of just action from the goals of all the other types of action. As we have seen, however, there is an ambiguity about the notion of art. It can apply to specific human activities like ship building and doctoring, or it can apply to the general activity of living life. In other words, it can apply either to the technical or to the moral sphere. In the following exchange, we will see how each party uses the ambiguous term "art."

Ch. 3 Popular Morality

THE EXAMINATION

Socrates asks whether those who have the art of being the best guards have also the art of being the best thieves.[8] He elaborates by asking whether the knowledge a doctor possesses in order to heal might not be turned equally to killing people efficiently. Polemarchus agrees that the knowledge necessary to these arts could be turned to either a good or an evil purpose. Guards have to know how thieves think and, on this basis, could make good thieves. And a doctor who knows how to cure will also know how to kill. Here, he acknowledges what any person of common sense must acknowledge; namely, that one may be an expert in a technical art and turn this knowledge to an evil purpose.

---

[8] See section 333e.

THE TRAP SPRINGS

Then, Socrates springs his trap. He notes that if justice is an art in the same way that guarding or healing is, then the most just person will have the capacity to be the most unjust. In other words, if justice is a kind of technical skill, then it can be turned to evil as easily as to good. Socrates then proceeds to cite several examples showing that there is a popular morality in which justice is considered to be a kind of technical skill. He cites the example of a great man who was famous throughout Greece for the artistry of his lying. This man was the father of Odysseus, whose keen wits were admired by all for their ability to protect friends and destroy enemies. Later on, Socrates notes that the notion of helping friends and harming enemies is most eminently practiced by tyrants and other powerful people. They are genuine artists at sorting out which people they should stick to as friends and which people they should stick it to as enemies.

POPULAR MORALITY

Socrates is putting his finger on what may be called popular morality, which tries to combine idealism with realism. Idealism is preached in order to reinforce the loyalty that should unite friends. Yet realism is also preached in order to enable friends to protect themselves against an outside enemy. There is a strong code of honor supporting this behavior of a group. Polemarchus' experience of trying to survive in the world has led him to define justice as if it were some kind of technical art. As we saw, a technical art can be turned either to a good or to a bad use. Hence, it serves as an example of popular morality, which admires the hero who is ready to give up his life for his friends or to butcher thousands of the enemy without mercy, all depending on what the code of the fraternity demands in the situation. To look at our own times, we want a President who will be as honest with Americans as a loving father but as crooked with the enemy as a used car salesman. We love the bomber pilot who will be kind to his pet dog, to his children, and to his beautiful wife and yet be ready to drop a nuclear bomb on the cities of our enemies. We will honor the CIA as long as the dirty tricks it practices abroad to confound our enemies are not turned upon Americans at home.

Expressed in the precise terms of Plato, popular morality considers justice to be a kind of technical skill, which enables its possessor to be loyal to friends but deadly to enemies.

THE EMBARRASSMENT OF POLEMARCHUS

Polemarchus, like most people would be, is embarrassed by seeing that the logical

Ch. 3 Popular Morality

conclusion drawn from his definition of justice is that the most just person is at the same time capable of being the most unjust. We might be equally embarrassed if someone implied that our loyalty to both friends and country made us capable of being disloyal and treacherous. While our common sense acknowledges that mere technical skill may be turned to evil purposes, it also acknowledges that really good persons are somehow solidified in their virtue: most unlikely to turn their gifts to an evil goal. In other words, while common sense may place justice in the category of being an art, it also distinguishes the art of justice from the technical arts.

Socrates expresses this commonsense conviction by concluding that one possessing the virtue of justice will not do harm to anyone. His reasoning is that because all arts enable their possessors to produce some good effect, so justice or virtue will enable their possessors to benefit other human beings, that is, to treat them justly or virtuously.

Thus, the initial definition of Polemarchus is turned upside down. Under the prodding of Socrates' questioning, the younger man moves from justice being the art of doing good to friends and harm to enemies to justice being the art of doing good to anyone with whom it comes in contact. For, as Socrates points out, if the art of herding is to benefit the herd and the art of healing is to benefit the patient, the art of justice is to benefit human beings.

POLEMARCHUS STUNG TO AWARENESS

Polemarchus has been stung into reevaluating his experience of life. Being a son of his father, Polemarchus adheres to the traditional notion of justice enough so as to be unwilling to apply it to successful tyrants. But being a child of his times, he cannot imagine that a truly just person would also be fair to his enemies. He, who once thought himself wise in these matters (rushing in to give his definition of justice) now begins to suspect that he might be ignorant. Consequently, in a turnabout that illustrates both his own nobility and his respect for Socrates, Polemarchus accepts the invitation of Socrates to continue further in their efforts to define justice.

CONCLUSION

In his portrayal of Polemarchus, Plato describes the type of person whose character is not entirely based upon his faithfulness to his natural knowledge of good and evil. The young man has been influenced by the ways of the world. Yet there is still a good deal of decency in the young man. He will admit that Socrates has caught him out in a contradiction. The fact that he makes this admission shows that he is capable of benefiting from the discipline of engaging in an intellectual inquiry for the nature of justice. This is possible only because the young man still has a respect for his conscience, for his knowledge of the natural law.

The point that Plato seems to be making is that intellectual training in the art of inquiry can be of benefit to a person who, though not solidly in the character of a virtuous person, still has enough respect for conscience to admit when he has contradicted himself. This is a very laudable quality. If inquirers have his type of humility, philosophy will be of some benefit to them if they practice it under a philosopher who is also a good person. In engaging in an inquiry into the nature of morality, they will unearth limitations in their own view of life and do something about them.

In this section, Plato is showing us how the intellectual tool of definition can be utilized for the purpose of moral instruction. It is part of man's natural knowledge to know that a good person is not an arrogant tyrant or supreme liar. But man does not always act

Ch. 3 Popular Morality

according to this knowledge and so may form a character motivated by popular morality, which has always loved a winner far more than a really good person. So powerful may the milieu be that people begin to forget that popular morality is not real morality. But if they attempt to define justice under the scrutiny of such a one as Socrates, they will soon be made conscious of how contradictory their view of justice is.

The reason they will see this contradiction, however, is that they really know better if they are forced to reflect upon the matter. This is often the goal of the Socratic investigation.

CHAPTER 4

ENTER THE ANTAGONIST

INTRODUCTION

In this chapter, we will discover yet another use of philosophy—that of shutting up or silencing someone who, refusing to be a partner in the discussion, chooses instead to be an opponent. The someone, in this case, is Thrasymachus, who, as we shall soon see, utterly despises the intellectual effort of Socrates and Polemarchus to reach a definition of justice. The reason is that Thrasymachus' views are radically antagonistic to those of all the others in the group.

The others take for granted that it is good to repay loans or to tell the truth and that it is evil to murder another or to tell lies. They may not have exactly the same philosophy of life, but they do have enough in common to at least embark upon the project of trying to define justice or virtue. But Thrasymachus is a revolutionary. One cannot assume that he takes the same view of murder, lying, and honesty, as do the others. Strictly speaking, then, he should not be allowed to join in the inquiry. For he is not in agreement with the others about the basic instances of what is just or virtuous and so cannot be expected to be of any help in defining the nature of justice or virtue.

Yet Plato does include this radical into his portrayal of a communal inquiry. His reason would seem to be that, although such people in theory have no place in such an inquiry, they usually dominate such inquiries in the real world with their loud and cynical talk. Plato, therefore, is interested in showing how

Ch. 4 Enter the Antagonist

Socrates, who is not only a good person but is also well trained in philosophy, handles the pseudo-intellectual who attempts to use reason to destroy the traditional sense of justice.

Thrasymachus will illustrate the type of person who maintains that life is really a jungle in which only the fittest survive. Thus, he has no use for anyone who takes the morality of the old man seriously. Nor does he have much more respect for the morality of Polemarchus, which, in his view, contains contradictions, which can be exploited by a skillful questioner like Socrates. But he despises Socrates most of all. The philosopher has used his formidable intellectual skills to suggest that justice may possibly be the art of doing good to all. Such cannot be the slogan of a "realist" trying to run an empire.

To some thinkers, the existence of a person like Thrasymachus is the perfect refutation of the natural law teaching that all men have a conscience and therefore a general sense of right and wrong simply by the fact that they are human beings. All we will say at this point is that the teaching does not hold that all men follow their conscience but only that they have one. Nor does this teaching require that all men profess to have a conscience; while all men have a conscience, a considerable portion of them seem to spend their whole lives denying this fact.

THRASYMACHUS ATTACKS

Thrasymachus enters the discussion with a bellow of impatience.[9] He has hardly been able to contain himself as he hears Socrates and Polemarchus trying to arrive at a definition of justice. He calls the participants idiots and dolts because of the earnestness and politeness of their exchange. He charges Socrates with playing his old game of always

---

[9] See section 336.

Ch. 4 Enter the Antagonist

posing questions but never giving any answers.

While the behavior of Thrasymachus may be boorish, it is not stupid. Thrasymachus is a veteran of the verbal battlefield at a time when democratic Athens was engaged in forging an empire against all comers. In such an atmosphere, the niceties of a debate in which the disputants dispassionately discuss the nature of justice would be considered a mere trick. For in the heart of men whose only concern is the acquisition of power lies the conviction that there is no such thing as an objective discussion; there is only the semblance of objectivity which manipulators of public opinion know how to assume for their own purposes. He therefore seeks to strip any disputant naked who tries to clothe himself in the robes of an objective judge. He attacks as a mere pose the fact that Socrates only asks questions but does not give a definition of his own. He challenges Socrates to say what justice is with clarity and precision, thus sparing his listeners from ponderous analogies involving duty, interest, profit, or advantage. These analogies produce only nonsense, says Thrasymachus, who has no time for such trash.

TOTAL WAR

Thrasymachus is employing a kind of *total war attack* against any claim that reason can arrive at a standard by which life should be lived. For justice, if discovered, would be such a standard. The very spectacle of two grown people seriously searching for "the right way to live" infuriates him. In his opinion, adults should know that in real life, the name of the game is power. According to him, might, not right, is what justice is all about.

Ch. 4 Enter the Antagonist

THE SOPHISTICATED RADICAL

Here, we have an example of a Sophisticated radical using his faculty of reason in order to destroy Reason. His view, as we shall soon see even more clearly, is that the only legitimate use of intelligence is to minister to the designs of power. Quite cleverly, then, he starts with ridiculing the person of Socrates, goes on to mock the give-and-take of inquiry, and finally belittles the use of analogy that Socrates constantly uses: making comparisons between the technical arts and the moral life in order to make a point about justice.

Thrasymachus objects to this practice.[10] Here, he seems to echo the common complaint that Socrates mixed his discussions about the high matter of politics with talk about carpenters and ship builders. The young Sophist is taking dead aim at all

---

[10] See section 336d.

the means that classical reason employs to make its points. If Socrates wilted under this attack, he would be forced to abandon the whole method of definition. For there is no way that justice can be defined if there is no give-and-take, if no analogy can be made between justice and the other arts.

Thrasymachus is a product of the new education based upon the teachings of the Sophists, who aimed to make their students skilled in the art of rhetoric and debate. Here, the object is to win a prize, not to find the truth. In brief, Thrasymachus is the type of political "realist" who speak today of playing hardball, of winning a person's heart by grabbing him in the right spot, and of negotiating from strength.

Ch. 4 Enter the Antagonist

SOCRATES' RESPONSE

But Socrates is no neophyte. In various ways, he quietly regains the ground that Thrasymachus is trying to cut out from under him. His most important ground, that of asking questions rather than giving answers, he regains by asking how anyone who admits his ignorance can be forced to give an answer. For it was the practice of Socrates to go around asking the Athenians questions because he admitted that he did not have the answers. Since so many others in the political realm seemed to be so sure of themselves, he felt that it was only right that he ask them questions and they give the answers. Is it not proper, he is saying, for the ignorant to seek wisdom from the wise?

NOT JUST IRONY

Certainly, there is irony in this reply of Socrates. Yet, he is quite serious about inquirers being ignorant. If they were not ignorant, how could they band together in order to look for the nature of justice? If they already knew it, why should they pretend to look for it? But this ignorance is only about the nature of justice in general. It cannot be about the experience of individual instances of what is just or right. It is not that he is ignorant that murder is wrong. If he has no conviction at all about this, then he is in no position to try to define justice. How can the reason of a person define that of which he has no experience? Not to hold that murder is evil is equivalent, on the moral level, to holding that there is no such thing as a house on the ordinary level of life.

The ignorance honored by Socrates is not total because the inquirers should have at least an experiential sense of what they are trying to define. The ticket of admission to any communal inquiry is not necessarily clear knowledge of the thing to be defined; it is some experience of that thing. It is this

Ch. 4 Enter the Antagonist

experience that provides the incentive for people to band together to get more knowledge of the thing in question.

Socrates is defending the right of those in the Human City (the community) to try to use reason when dealing with political or social matters. Thrasymachus scorns this very attempt. People like Thrasymachus despise the notion that citizens can try to settle deep differences in their own experiences by trying to use their reason in an objective way. To him, the only legitimate use of reason is to advance the cause of power, not to discover any such thing as the truth.

In principle, the Sophist is opposed to any effort to take the process of definition seriously. For the very process obviates those long speeches and harangues by which a debater appeals to emotion and prejudice rather than to reason. In using the rather dry process of definition, Socrates is trying to protect reason, a most delicate faculty easily damaged by the passions unleashed by political differences.

THE DEBATE

There are many exchanges in the long debate between Socrates and Thrasymachus. But we will only give a sample of the first in order to give the flavor of the whole. The young man begins only after the group assures him that they will take up a collection to pay him for his efforts. He is like the hired professional who springs to life only when his pocket is filled. With great assurance, he defines justice as simply the interest of the stronger.[11]

To grasp the logic of the following exchange, we can expand this definition of justice to being 'the art whereby the strong protect their interests.' As we mentioned before, the common assumption of all the

---

[11] See section 338c.

inquirers is that justice or virtue is some kind of an art. Thrasymachus is saying in effect that the genus of justice is art and the differentia, which separates the art of justice from all the other arts, is the fact that it is used by the strong. Under questioning, he clarifies his statement, saying that the stronger are the ruling class. In democracies it is the people; in tyrannies, the tyrant; in aristocracies, the aristocrats. In other words, the laws of any regime are fashioned to protect the· powers of the rulers. In democracy, these are the many. In aristocracy, they are the few. And in monarchy, it is the one. There is indeed something very modern (and very ancient) about the way in which Thrasymachus describes the various ways that political power is distributed and exercised.

THE STRATEGY OF SOCRATES

Socrates has already recognized that his moral experience has nothing in common with the young man's. There is really, then, no proper ground for conducting an inquiry. Yet Socrates does not allow the young man to take over the field by means of his long invectives, thus allowing political discussions to be merely an exchange between various speakers attacking others from their own soap boxes. Appealing to a general sense of fairness, he had previously prodded the young man into giving his own definition. In doing so, Thrasymachus tacitly admits that justice must be some kind of an art. Whether he wants to or not, then, he is taking his stand on a notion, which is not his invention but is a common possession of the culture. For the notion of an art does have some common meaning that is not at the arbitrary whim of any person who uses that term. The upcoming battle, then, does have its rules. It will be up to Thrasymachus to show that his notion of justice does fit the general notion of being an art. Is it up to Socrates to examine this notion in the light of experience to see whether it holds up?

DO RULERS MAKE MISTAKES?[12]

Socrates' first question is whether rulers ever make mistakes. Taking a commonsense view of the question, Thrasymachus agrees that they do. Socrates then points out that if a ruler makes a mistake in a particular case, justice in that case will be for the benefit of the ruled, of the weaker. If that is the case, Socrates urges, then the young man's definition is wrong. For if in some cases it works out that justice, the absolute obedience which subjects owe to their rulers, results in benefiting the weak to the detriment of the strong, then it cannot be universally true that justice is the art safeguarding the interest of the strong.

---

[12] See section 339c.

THE ERUPTION[13]

At this point the party erupts. Polemarchus agrees with the logic of Socrates, and many of the others side with Thrasymachus. In a long speech designed to make Socrates look like a silly nitpicker, Thrasymachus points out that, when he speaks of a ruler, he means the ruler *qua* ruler. Based upon the common agreement that ruling is an art, he argues that the expert as expert never makes a mistake. In the real world, we all know that experts make mistakes. But the point is that experts cannot make mistakes due to their art; the mistakes must be because they sometimes forget their art.

Socrates is perfectly willing to admit that rulers as rulers never make mistakes. In fact, he encourages such precise use of terms, dryly commenting that Thrasymachus

---

[13] See section 340.

Ch. 4 Enter the Antagonist

should always stick to such high standards. Here Socrates has made Thrasymachus go on record that the term 'art' is to be understood by all in the strict sense that its practitioner always does the right thing.

THE KILL

In the next series of passages, Socrates moves in for the kill. Citing the other arts as examples, he gets Thrasymachus to admit that the goal of an art is not the perfection of the art itself, which is already a perfect thing, but the production of some product out of raw or imperfect material. For example, the goal of the art of shipbuilding is take some material and make a ship out of it. The goal of the art of medicine is take a sick person and make him well. The goal of the art of sheep herding is to raise and protect sheep that would otherwise be helpless. In all these cases, the purpose of the art is for the sake of the product, not for the sake of the art itself.

To put the matter more pointedly, the direct object of medicine is to cure the sick, not to line the pockets of the doctor.

Consequently, justice cannot be the art which benefits the strong, the ruler. It must be the art which, though it is possessed by the strong, is used to benefit the weak, the real object of the art. In other words, the art of ruling should be for the sake of the ruled. By his questioning, Socrates has forced Thrasymachus to reverse his position totally. Instead of justice being the art whose end is the benefit of the strong, it is now the art whose goal is the benefit of the weak.[14]

THE REACTION OF THE YOUNG SOPHIST

The young man is furious at this turn of the argument, which has taken place in front of an audience whom he had so arrogantly

---

[14] See section 342e.

Ch. 4 Enter the Antagonist

addressed in the beginning. He is not very grateful for having been stung. But he controls himself and picks up again on his former mode of attacking the person of the questioner instead of addressing the issue itself. He asks whether Socrates, probably a good twenty years older than himself, has a nurse. He explains his question by suggesting that Socrates is like some snot-nosed kid running around free of his nanny. He amplifies on the theme of his opponent's innocence by pointing out that real rulers in life are like real shepherds—both spend night and day thinking up new ways to fleece their flocks. The young man roars on with a long speech and then makes a move to leave the gathering.

But Socrates gets him to stay, and the debate goes on for many more pages. Socrates relentlessly pushes on, requiring Thrasymachus to give a real intellectual account of his views instead of poisoning the air with invective, harangue, mockery, and long speeches. Step by step, Socrates patiently examines with questions the contention of Thrasymachus that the just are foolish, ignorant, and weak, showing instead that they are sensible, wise and strong.

The young man is not convinced but he is silenced. At one point, he even turns red in the face[15] as if embarrassed by the sheer perversity and shamelessness of his own assertions. Here we seem to have an indirect proof of natural law teaching, namely, that man cannot totally corrupt his natural knowledge of good and evil. There will always be some sense, even in the totally vicious person, that they have done evil.

FINAL OUTCOME

At the very end of Book One, Plato portrays Socrates as expressing dissatisfaction with the whole previous inquiry and

---

[15] See section 350d.

Ch. 4 Enter the Antagonist

then explaining why. Socrates blames himself for being like an overanxious diner rushing around the banquet snatching at various foods instead of settling down to the main course. For the main course was to consist in a definition of justice itself, as is indicated by the question that initiated the whole feast of words. Socrates however has been distracted from attempting an answer to the question because he has been busy examining the answers volunteered by the younger men, who quite hastily rushed into the inquiry with their own opinions. He has been busy dealing with the way that justice appears to others rather than the way it exists in itself.

Now, Socrates himself cannot be blamed for this failure. Trained in the courtesies of inquiry, he has not brushed aside the proposals of the others to present his own. Rather, he has carefully examined their proposals and shown why they are deficient. What else could he do? But the net result is negative rather than positive. It shows us definitions that do not work, but not the definition of justice itself.

REFLECTION

At this juncture, the conclusion of Book One, it might be appropriate to reflect upon what Plato has told us. He seems to be telling us that there are times in human affairs, times of crisis, in which people are confused about what is right or wrong. They no longer have the certainties of their forefathers, of people like the old man Cephalus. Yet, they are not quite ready to embrace the radical views of men like Thrasymachus. At this point, Socrates and later Plato enter upon the scene, trying to defend the old religious certainties in a philosophical way.

The Sophists have used the sharp tools of logic to dismantle traditional morality. Plato will use those same tools to build it up. He will rehabilitate reason, intellectual endeavor, the scientific method, and the philosophical

Ch. 4 Enter the Antagonist

way. He will enlist them in the aid of religion and of natural law thinking. We have already seen him at work in this regard. By the use of the question-and-answer technique, he has shown how philosophy may be used to reveal to a person that their moral views involve contradictions. He has also shown how philosophy can be used to shut up a clever opponent by sticking to the point rather than being confused by all the tricks of an opponent who is trying to use reason merely to muddy the issue.

But does philosophy have any other uses? It would seem that it does. Plato will begin to show us that in Book Two.

CHAPTER 5

THE BASIC QUESTION

INTRODUCTION

In this chapter, we will see Plato begin his task of showing us the main work of philosophy. That work will be to delineate precisely what justice is in itself. What do we mean by the expression "in itself"? To answer that, let us go back to our definition of house. There are many different ways one can consider individual houses. Writers can see them as homes for a family and so write poems or novels about them. Builders can consider their construction as a means of making a living and so write technical manuals about them. Governments can see them as sources of revenue and so write tax laws about them. The experiences that human beings have of houses are practically infinite in variety. But when a philosopher looks at an individual house, he is trying to grasp its essential or fundamental features. He is trying to understand what a house is in itself, not in the many ways it can appear to different people. In short, he is trying to grasp the nature of house. So, too, when one is trying to determine the nature of justice, one is treating it as it exists in itself and, consequently, independently of any particular way that people might see it.

There is a quality of timelessness and immutability about the definition of a thing in itself. Though particular houses may change with time, their definition does not. For the definition articulates the essential features of a house. If the definition should change, then the thing defined would no

Ch. 5 The Basic Question

longer be a house. If one changed the definition of man from being a rational to an irrational animal, we would no longer have a man—we would have a brute. The definition of an object derives from the object itself, and thus, cannot change (even if there were no houses, the *nature* of house still exists).

Applying this point to the matter of justice itself, we see that the task of Plato is to take the experience of the good man as his foundation and then to delineate its essentials or fundamentals. In other words, Plato will consider the religious views of such a man as Cephalus and show how they all fit together into an orderly whole. If Plato has really grasped the essentials of this religious experience, these essentials have a timeless and immutable quality. They also have a universal quality. Just as the definition of the nature of an individual house applies to all houses, so the definition of the nature of an individual's religious experience applies to all religious experiences of that type.

The Right Way to Live

To put the matter more concretely, the task of Plato is to take the experience of the old man—how he did not worry about morality in his youth, how his former sins began to haunt him in his age, how he would wake up at night with fears about his soul, how he would devote his later years to sacrificing to the gods and giving restitution to those he offended—and to translate these particular experiences into universal categories which apply to all mankind and are timeless. Though the knowledge of these abstract categories lacks the warmth and color of the individual experiences from which they are drawn, it enables one to defend one's convictions. For Plato is not speaking in personal terms, which his opponents may reject as mere private opinion. He is speaking in universal and timeless terms, which claim to be the truth. His opponents may still reject his view but now they are compelled to give their own reasons, which of course cannot be merely private opinions but must also represent universal claims. In debates taking place in the public square, the issue should move from the level of individual experience to that of universal truth.

To many a modern thinker, all of the above statements are obviously and shockingly false. He does not hold that there are realities that have a definite nature or identity, which allow them to be defined. If he admits the possible existence of such realities, he denies that the human mind has the ability to understand them. And if he admits that the human mind can understand such realities, it is because they are not realities in themselves but are merely creations of the human mind. A modern thinker could not and would not take the project of trying to define justice very seriously. In fact, he does not hold that there is really any truth to be found in debates about justice but, like Thrasymachus, would consider such debates to be a noble cover for hiding self-interest.

INTRODUCING BOOK TWO

Let us now proceed to the task of introducing Book Two. The best way is to analyze the way in which Plato himself introduces it. Being the artist he is, he communicates essential matters merely by placing certain words in the mouths of certain speakers. The essential matter he is dealing with is the structure of the whole inquiry, which depends upon the question that initiates it. He puts this basic question into the mouth of a young man, Glaucon, who is a companion of Socrates and an older brother of Plato.

Let us examine the setting in which Glaucon asks his question. At the very beginning of Book Two,[16] Glaucon announces that he will not let the inquiry die. He thinks that Thrasymachus has given up too easily and should have put up a better

---

[16] See section 357a.

Ch. 5 The Basic Question

fight. Therefore, he, Glaucon, will state the case of the Sophist with all the power he can muster. At first, the reader might be surprised that a friend of Socrates can take up the side of Thrasymachus so vigorously. Can it be that he shares the same view as the young radical? He does not! Glaucon's basic sympathies are with Socrates who, as we saw, favors the religious views of the old man. Nevertheless, the youth confesses that his ears have been flooded in the public square with the type of opinions expressed by Thrasymachus. Though he does not agree with these views, he does not have the intellectual ability to refute them.

Here, I believe we have a perfect model for many decent young people today. Their hearts are in the right place, but they are being bombarded by a culture antagonistic to their real convictions. They are looking for answers that will justify their convictions. In the case of Glaucon, his situation prompts him to seek help from Socrates. He asks the older man a key question. The answer to that question will take up the rest of *The Republic*, which supplies the classic philosophical view supporting the notion of justice. Young adults today, particularly Catholics, should examine the answers supplied by traditional philosophy, which has always held an honored place in the teaching mission of the Catholic Church.

THE QUESTION OF GLAUCON

Glaucon's question comes out of his experience of the basic conflict between two views of life. The first view comes from his traditional training in religion, which maintains that virtue or justice are sacred things in themselves, and therefore are blessed by the gods and should be honored by man. The fact that justice is a sacred thing is the reason why it is blessed and honored. It is not the fact that it is blessed and honored that makes justice an essentially worthy thing. It is

Ch. 5 The Basic Question

worthy or valuable in itself. The second comes from his exposure to political life, and is the view of Thrasymachus; namely, that justice is not a sacred, worthy, or valuable thing in itself, which therefore should be honored by all men. Rather, it is an instrument or tool, which receives its value from the fact that the powerful use it to protect their own interests.

The precise question flowing from a comparison of these two views is this: what is the nature of justice? Is it a good to be sought both for its own sake and for its consequences? Clearly this concept of justice arises from a religious tradition, which insists that justice is a noble or sacred thing in itself which, if honored, also brings blessings to man. Here, justice is intrinsically noble or sacred.

Or is justice to be defined as merely a useful good? Defining justice in this way may not seem all that bad to many readers because they see that the law, for example, is very useful for maintaining order in society. Later, we will examine this notion in more detail. It is enough for our purposes now to interpret this notion in the context of how Thrasymachus sees justice; namely, as a thing of sheer power which the strong in society use to protect their own interests.

In other words, is justice to be loved as something that is valuable in itself, an intrinsic good? Or is it merely a useful good? Socrates answers that it is intrinsic. Glaucon, speaking not for himself but for the Sophist, answers that it is merely useful.

Again, we should note that the reader may not yet see the full force of the contrast between justice as an intrinsic good and as a useful good. To appreciate fully what Plato means by so strongly opposing these notions, however, the reader will have to follow the argument as it develops.

Glaucon then goes on to present the views of the Sophist with all the wit and eloquence he can muster. He wants to make sure that

Ch. 5 The Basic Question

Socrates, in trying to refute these views, will be dealing with the same difficulties that have troubled him and other young people when encountering the debates in the public square. In brief, the young man is looking for a champion among his elders who can give an intellectual justification and defense of religious tradition.

AN IMPORTANT PRINCIPLE

The portrayal of Glaucon embodies a very important principle. In depicting Glaucon as a friend of Socrates, Plato is indicating that the young man is already a good person. Hence, the author continues to assert that before one can define justice, the right way to live, one must already have the experiential knowledge to understand and the solid character to follow the right way. This accords with the general observation we have lain down earlier; namely, that before one can embark upon defining the nature of a house, one must already have experience of the individual thing.

And before one can do a good job in building a house, one must have had enough practice to have acquired the necessary skill. In applying this rule to moral matters, we see that the experience deals with recognizing and doing good and noble deeds. The only type of person who has this experience is the person with a solid character. Only such people will know as a matter of fact that certain deeds are just and others are unjust. Only such people will be able to do the one and avoid the other as naturally as other people breathe. They will not need long and involved arguments to see that, for example, it is a good and noble thing for a soldier to give one's life for his fellow man. Later, Aristotle will say that the student of moral philosophy must be well-habituated in the ways of morality so that, before he learns *why* certain actions are good or evil, he will know *that* they are good and evil.

Ch. 5 The Basic Question

Putting the matter another way, we can say that one wishing to philosophize about the right way to live cannot be a neutral observer or a detached critic of the moral scene. One must already be committed to living the right way. Here, the tradition of Plato is in direct contradiction to the modern view that the philosopher must approach all moral questions with "open-mindedness." So prevalent is this modern view that students of a reflective turn of mind might think that the study of philosophy will show them the right way to live. At the conclusion of the course, they often end up being more skeptical than they were in the beginning. As Newman says in *The Idea of a University*, human reason is too delicate an instrument to be able to deal by itself with those giants, the passion and the pride of man. Reason needs the proper experience as the foundations for its reflection.

To summarize: our first analysis of the basic question has shown us that the question, being philosophical in nature, does not imply that the one questioning is ignorant about its answer experientially. One is only ignorant of how to state the answer philosophically.

NOT ENTIRELY IGNORANT

Yet we are not entirely ignorant even of the philosophical answer. If we analyze the question that Glaucon has asked, we will see that he already knows a good deal about how to reach the answer to his own question. The question is whether justice is an intrinsic or merely a useful good. First, he knows that there is such a thing as justice. One cannot ask whether justice is of one type or the other without assuming that there is such a thing as justice.

One assumes this on the basis of their practical experience. Second, the young man already knows the nature of both intrinsic and useful goods. Otherwise, he could not have asked whether it was the nature of justice to be one or the other. Third, he already knows, in a general way, something about the nature of goodness. Otherwise, he could not have asked whether justice was one type of good or another.

What we have seen is that, by the very fact that one asks a question, one is expressing a great deal of knowledge not just doubt. The next section will illustrate how Glaucon already knows the nature of both intrinsic and useful goods.

WHAT THE TEXT SHOWS

The text[17] shows that before Glaucon asks the basic question, he points out the existence of three types of goods. He describes goods, which are different from each other, not accidentally or superficially, but essentially or fundamentally. The first are goods which are

---

[17] See section 357b.

pleasurable: if one desires a thing simply for its own sake without any regard for its consequences, then that thing is a pleasurable good. Games, amusements, luxury foods—anything that produces a pleasant sensation fits under this category. As far as the definition of justice is concerned, this category can be disregarded, for no one has considered it as a pleasurable good.

If one desires a thing both for its own sake and its consequences, then we have the second type of good: the intrinsic. It is valued both for itself and for the consequences it brings upon its possessor. Health and knowledge fit under this category. One can seek health both because a healthy body is valuable in itself and because it enables a person to work more efficiently. One can seek knowledge both because the truth is loved for its own sake and because it enables a person to get a job. Earlier, we described this type of good as being noble or sacred.

Finally, we have the third type of good. If one desires a thing only for its consequences, then that thing is a useful good. Taking bitter medicine, having a leg amputated, or enduring hard labor are of such a type. They are not valued for any intrinsic worth they may have; in fact, they are often feared as evils. Nevertheless, they are sought by people wishing to retain their health, save their lives, or make a living. We also call them necessary evils.

THE POINT OF THESE DISTINCTIONS

The point of these distinctions is quite clear: they establish in the mind of the inquirer the precise meaning of what is meant by intrinsic and useful goods. Keeping this idea in mind, the inquirers are then to examine their own experiences of life for the sake of categorizing them. Would they, for example, place the just deed of giving one's life for another under the category of intrinsic or useful? If they do not have a very clear idea of these general categories, then they will not be able to examine their own experience with any precision.

Another function of these distinctions is to present the opposition between the two notions of justice as precisely as possible. If justice is an intrinsic good, then it must be valuable in itself. But if justice is merely a useful good, then it has value solely for its capacity to be used to attain something that is good in itself. It is a necessary evil, which a person may seek in order to avoid a greater evil. We can be sure that there is an opposition between the two notions that does not leave any middle ground. Since we have eliminated the category of pleasurable good as a place in which to put justice, we are left with only two categories which are absolutely opposed to each other: what is good in itself and what is not good in itself but only useful. By thus opposing the notions of justice, Plato ensures that there will be a very definite clash of two forces, a definite distinction between two possible choices. Such a sharp distinction makes for a good intellectual drama in which there is going to be a definite winner and a definite loser at the end and not some wishy-washy conclusion in which everybody is right in a way but also wrong in a way.

THE NOTION OF GOODNESS

Let us now reexamine the basic question so that we may see the third thing (the notion of goodness) that Glaucon understands in a preliminary way. Clearly, he must have some understanding of the notion of goodness because he is asking whether justice is an intrinsic or a useful good. This situation is similar to one we have met in previous chapters. There, we saw how the process of definition always begins with placing the thing to be defined in some general category and then narrowing that category down. In Book One of *The Republic*, Socrates and his companions took for granted that justice must be some kind of an art. In Book Two, the inquirers are taking for granted that it must be some kind of a good. Here Glaucon does not explain in any detail this very interesting and vitally important notion. But let us investigate it for ourselves. If we wish to get to the bottom of things, if we wish to make secure our intellectual footing, then we have to look more closely at this notion by trying to define it. For it will be in understanding this notion that we will discover the most important principle of all in our inquiry into the nature of justice.

THE PROCESS OF DEFINING GOOD IN GENERAL

To define the notion of good, we must approach it in the same way as any other thing we are trying to define; namely, we must first reflect upon our experience of the individual instances of the thing in question.

Ch. 5 The Basic Question

In the case of goodness, we reflect upon the various ways in which we use the term. We speak of good people and deeds, using the term in its moral sense. But we also speak of good athletes and works of art. And we also speak of good ice creams, candies, plants, pets, and medicines. In fact, when we think about it, there are very few things (if any) that we or someone else in this wide world might not call a good. We might not consider murdering someone a good deed, but a murderer might.

The next step in the defining process is, as we saw earlier, to see if there is any one characteristic that is common in all the individual ways we have used the term. In other words, what do human beings, deeds, ice-creams, athletes, rocks, and pets have in common when we call them good? The answer is that they are desirable in some way. In other words, they are things which are either actual or possible objects of human desire. Put in classic terms, a thing is good when it serves as the end or goal of a human activity, which, after all, is the expression of human desire.

DEFINING JUSTICE

In defining justice in a preliminary way as being some type of good, we see that it is an end or goal of human action. Thus, justice (whether intrinsic or useful) is good simply because it is desired by men. This is true, but it is also trivial. No one debates whether the types of justice are good in a general sense. Of course, they are. They are at least good in the same way as murder or rape is so. They are desirable to at least some people. Otherwise, they would not be done. But what people do debate about is whether a just deed has intrinsic or sacred value or whether it has only extrinsic or practical value.

If one maintains that justice is an intrinsic good, he will also maintain that justice sought only as a useful good is a morally evil pursuit.

Ch. 5 The Basic Question

On the other hand, if one maintains that justice is merely a useful good, he will also maintain that doing good deeds for their own sake is the mark of a fool. On a practical or experiential level, very few people would have difficulty in judging which attitude is morally good and which is morally evil. Indeed, if you meet up with a person who has trouble making this judgment, you would do well to give them a very wide berth! But on a philosophical level, it is not so easy to pin down exactly *why* the one deed is good and the other evil. This is the problem we are concerned with.

ANY HIGHEST END?

This problem can be solved if there is indeed a highest end or good which is the goal of all human activity. Then, the activities that promote this goal, are morally good, meaning that they perfect or complete the human being as a human being. And those activities, which detract from the goal, are morally evil, meaning that they corrupt the human being as human being. To put the matter another way: the problem will be solved if the human activity called living has a purpose. Then the activities, which attain this purpose, will be morally good, and those, which frustrate it, will be morally evil. Here, we are not speaking of the purpose or goal of some particular agent like a shoemaker or trumpet player, or shepherd. A person can be a good shoemaker, trumpet player, or shepherd without necessarily being a good human being. Here, we are speaking of the goal of the human being as an end or good, which completes or perfects his very humanity. Is there any such goal? If there is, its attainment will serve as the objective standard by which we can determine which notion of justice is the moral one.

Ch. 5 The Basic Question

THE GOAL OF HAPPINESS

Aristotle, the famous pupil of Plato, answers this question by saying that all people seem to agree that the goal of human life is the attainment of happiness. What Aristotle maintained in the past is still true today. This point can be seen from the fact that if we examine why human beings act, we will see that they always act, without exception, in order to be happy. Saints and sinners, Good Samaritans and serial killers, martyrs and suicides all act for the sake being happy, which in some cases may mean avoiding great pain. As our examples suggest, however, people do not agree on the nature of happiness. And it is this disagreement that sets off Aristotle's philosophical quest for the right way to live. The disagreement centers around the question of the nature or definition of happiness. This makes sense because one can only tell what actions are right or wrong when one knows what the goal of human actions should be.

Here, Aristotle is simply making explicit what is already implicit in the speech of Glaucon. What the young man is really asking is who will be happier? Will it be a Socrates holding that justice is an intrinsic good, thus defining good as the decent or honorable thing to do simply because it is decent or honorable? Or will it be a Sophist holding that it is only a useful good, thus defining good as having value only because it is opportune or beneficial to the doer in promoting his own interests. This is the basic question of the *whole Republic* stated most precisely. As we have been trying to point out in this chapter, the fact that Glaucon (or indeed anyone who has thought through the process outlined in this chapter) has a solid grasp of the elements involved in the question means that he is fully equipped to enter into a communal inquiry into its answer.

Ch. 5 The Basic Question

REVIEW OF
THE THREE REASONS WHY

A review of the three reasons why is as follows.

1. In asking the question, Glaucon already has the proper experience from which he will draw his answer. This experience is not supplied by his study of philosophy, but by his having chosen to form a character which reflects a proper upbringing. A person without this experience is one who has no knowledge at all of individual houses, either in reality or in imagination, and yet is trying to define the nature of house.

2. The young man has a precise understanding of the terms *good*, *intrinsic*, and *useful*. These are the general categories which will contain the specific notions of justice and injustice. Unless one has a precise grasp of the general categories, one cannot locate with precision what lies within them. This grasp comes from intellectual training,

which makes explicit and precise what the student already knows implicitly and vaguely.

3. The most important principle in the whole project of determining what is morally right or wrong is that happiness is the objective standard. The degree to which the inquirer understands the specific nature of happiness is the degree to which he will be able to determine the proper definition of justice. This grasp comes from the proper philosophical training.

UNIVERSAL AND TIMELESS TRUTH

We have seen, in the beginning of the chapter, that even in the definition of a house we are in possession of a universal and timeless truth. All the more will we have such a truth if we are able to define justice? We have not yet done so. Yet we are already in possession of such a truth when we know that happiness is the highest goal of human activity. This is indeed a most general and

Ch. 5 The Basic Question

even vague truth. But it is certain. We should then be able to start our inquiry by taking such a general but certain truth and applying it to our experience of life. The more that we can fill in this outline with details from our experience, the more specific will our knowledge of justice be. Just as the experienced carpenter is able to fill in with specifics the general knowledge that we all have of the nature of a house, so will the good and experienced person be able to fill in with specifics the general notion we all have of happiness and of justice.

Most modem thinkers do not accept the starting points from which we, under the guidance of Plato, are beginning our inquiry. The modern reader has two tasks to accomplish. The first is that of following the argument between Socrates and the Sophist. This, all readers throughout history have had to accomplish. The second is that of following the argument between the ancient and the modern philosophers. Plato holds that there are objective and universal truths about the right way to live. In other words, he holds that there are norms of morality, which are absolute, objective, and unchanging. Most modern thinkers, on the contrary, hold that norms of morality are relative, subjective, and evolve with history. Now, Catholics should hold, at least by faith, that there are moral absolutes which do not change with the times. The question is whether it can be proved by philosophical reason alone that there are such norms. I mention this point to illustrate that in reading *The Republic* one is entering into a debate not just with those in the past but with many in the present. In fact, the debate itself is universal and timeless.

CHAPTER 6

THE VIEW OF THE SOPHIST

INTRODUCTION

In the last chapter, we saw that Glaucon seems to have had a great deal of intellectual training: he introduced the basic question with a great deal of philosophical precision. In this chapter, we will see that Glaucon also seems to have had a great deal of experience in the public square listening to many orators trained in the new school of the Sophists: he will elaborate on the basic question in such a slanted way as to make it seemingly impossible for Socrates to answer it. In short, Glaucon will use all the rhetorical tricks that have been used on him. When the young man tried to defend what was decent and noble, he was made to look like a fool by those mouthing the dominant themes of his culture. He is in no mood to serve up soft questions to his master, Socrates. He wants to see his champion erect a solid philosophical structure, which can house and defend the experience of the man led by conscience.

RECALLING THE BASIC PRINCIPLE

Before proceeding, let's review the basic principles which will dictate the structure of Glaucon's speech and indeed the speech of anyone who is trying to define the nature of justice. As indicated in the previous chapter, the very question which the inquirers are asking already shows what they take for granted and about what they are disputing. The question is: Is it the pursuit of justice as an intrinsic or as a useful good that leads to happiness? We see how those asking this question accept three statements as obviously

Ch. 6 The View of the Sophist

true. First, the most basic truth: happiness, being man's highest goal, is the objective standard by which the right notion of justice is discovered. As we have already seen, the goal of an activity determines the type of activity which attains it. One's notion of happiness will determine one's notion of how to get it.

The second truth is that one must then show how the pursuit of a particular notion of justice will lead to the attainment of happiness, thus showing that the notion is the right one. One must also show how the pursuit of the opposing notion of justice will lead to unhappiness, thus showing that it is the wrong one.

The third truth is that all the contestants must draw evidence for their positions from man's ordinary experience of life. For actual experience is the court in which the truth of all general notions are tested. This, then, is the intellectual procedure, which all the participants in the inquiry must follow.

THE MATTER UNDER DISPUTE

As we noted above, the question asked by the inquirers also indicates the matter upon which they are disputing. This matter is the precise nature of justice. How will this matter be settled by each inquirer? It will be settled when each establishes the connection between the right notion of happiness and the proper notion of justice by drawing upon their experience of life. In other words, each inquirer will move intellectually from what is accepted as true (the starting points) to what has been in doubt (the conclusion).

How will the matter be settled by the group? It will be settled when a review of the ordinary human experience of life shows that one view promotes while the other impedes the attainment of happiness. If any inquirer rejects any of these elements, he cannot take part in the communal effort to define justice. He is outside the process because he does not hold the truth of the starting points which all

Ch. 6 The View of the Sophist

must accept as evident. In brief, he cannot be philosophically rational in these matters because he has rejected the very principles which human reason needs to conduct an inquiry into the truth about the right way to live.

Most moderns reject the possibility of attaining truth in these matters, holding that human reason can move with certitude only in matters of physical science and mathematics. This view is reflected in the modern university, where both faculty and students consider that the talk above, about reason, truth, and basic principles, is merely a matter of opinion which was once taken for truth by the ancients but is no longer pertinent to modern conditions. This is the modern dogma whose truth is taken as self-evident by most intellectuals today. Hardly anyone questions it. But we are doing just that. We are asking if they are correct. The only way we can answer that question is to attempt to reason the matter through for ourselves.

Natural law philosophers like Plato, Aristotle, and St. Thomas claim to know the answer because they have reasoned the matter out. We may quite legitimately accept their word for it. But then we will be exercising faith, not reason. If we wish to make this claim upon the basis of reason, then we must travel the road of reason. There are no shortcuts—the way is long and even rather dull. But that is because we are rational animals and hence must proceed step-by-step in our reasoning. We are not angels, who can see complex matters all in one glance.

THE SPEECH OF GLAUCON

Let us now begin with the text. Glaucon proposes to begin at the beginning; he lays out an analysis of justice by depicting its origin and nature.[18] He immediately lays down the sophist principle that it is naturally

---

[18] See section 358e.

Ch. 6 The View of the Sophist

good for people to do injustice but naturally bad for them to suffer it. A little later on, he expands on this point, saying that the very best thing in life is to be able to do injustice with impunity and that the very worst thing is to suffer injustice without being able to take revenge.

Glaucon is actually laying down the particular notion of happiness, which will serve as the standard by which he will judge the proper notion of justice. According to the Sophist, happiness consists of the exercise of perfect freedom (liberty), which is defined as being able to do whatever one wishes without any fear of interference. The corollary is that the greatest evil in life is the inability to do whatever one wishes because one is enslaved by some superior power. Here, we have a depiction of the highest goal of human nature according to the Sophist and, therefore, the standard by which he will judge what is morally good and what is morally evil. Since the Sophist holds that justice is to be defined as a useful good, it is then up to him to show the necessary connection between his notion of justice and his notion of happiness by citing the evidence supplied by man's experience of life.

MAN'S EXPERIENCE

In describing this experience, Glaucon depicts a time in which human beings supposedly lived in a state in which there was no such thing as government or law. In this state of affairs, however, the majority soon discovered that they very rarely attained their highest good but instead most often suffered their worst evil. Only a minority had the strength to exercise total freedom. This state was supposed to be *natural* for man.

Eventually, the majority determined to improve their lot by drawing up a contract or making a bargain among themselves. They would give up their right to perfect liberty (which they rarely got anyway) in order to

Ch. 6 The View of the Sophist

avoid suffering their greatest evil—total enslavement. This compact was a compromise between the greatest good and the greatest evil; a bargain that was the origin of government and law, from which the notion of justice was born. It would now be the function of the government to protect the majority from the strong. In brief, then, justice would be an instrument or tool created by human beings as a means of avoiding the greatest of evils. It would not be natural to man. Being a construct of reason, it would be artificial. No one would like the notion of justice itself—it would detract from perfect liberty. As such, it would be an evil and would never be chosen for its own sake. Yet, people would still choose it because, evil as it was, it would still be less evil than a total loss of liberty. It would be a necessary evil. Here, of course, we have the notion of justice merely as a useful good. People use justice to escape slavery just as people amputate their legs to avoid death.

QUITE ACCEPTABLE

The ordinary person, perhaps a follower of popular morality, might well feel that the theory of justice outlined above is the right notion. He will admit that he often obeys the law only to avoid the penalties for breaking it. As an American, he will accept the theory that the people have created the government by a compact in which they have given it some of their natural liberties to attain its protection. For the theory of justice laid out by the Sophist is practically the same theory that political scientists today accept as the basis for the modern liberal democracy. As a practical man with a good sense of how the world functions, he will have no difficulty with the notion of justice being a useful good.

But this ordinary person might begin to feel uneasy as he listens to the Sophist develop his ideas further. The Sophist makes the blanket assertion that no one at all would abide by the law if he had the power to escape

Ch. 6 The View of the Sophist

it. To the ordinary man this might seem like too radical a statement, one that a wild man like Thrasymachus might make. Yet, here the Sophist is simply drawing out logically the implication of calling justice a merely useful good. The implication is that if one can attain his goal without using any tool or instrument, he clearly will not use one. The Sophist is aware of this uneasiness on the part of more conventional people. But he will have none of that reaction, feeling that it is hypocritical. He tells a tale whose whole point is to stem any moral outrage his listeners might vent on him. He tells them the tale of the Ring of Gyges.

THE TALE

There was a shepherd named Gyges, who discovered a ring, which gave him the power to become invisible. Delighted with this ring, he then volunteered to present the monthly report to the King and the Queen, the owners of the flocks that he tended. Using the power of the ring, he soon managed to seduce the Queen and then kill the King, thereby making himself the new ruler of the land.

Here, the Sophist is pointing out that if individuals somehow lose their fear of punishment by acquiring their own Ring of Gyges, they will disregard justice because it will no longer be useful to them. In this view there is no fundamental difference between people. They will all break the law if they can get away with it. The superficial difference between them—the difference between the so-called good people and the reputedly evil ones is that the former are not powerful or creative enough to break the law while the latter are.

In telling this story, the Sophist feels that he is unmasking the shallow hypocrisy of people like Polemarchus, who think they can be respectable and yet consider justice merely as a useful good. The Sophist may also feel that he is exposing the emptiness of the

Ch. 6 The View of the Sophist

Socratic position with the assertion that no human being will respect justice given the opportunity to disregard it with impunity. The story fashioned by the Sophist then is a very powerful way of revealing the hearts of men.

THE GERAGHTY RING COMPANY

When I was teaching this tale to a class of collegians, who were involved at the time in getting their junior rings, I announced that I had recently founded a new enterprise called the Geraghty Ring Company. My rings would be very expensive, I announced, but they would be worth it—they would have the same power as the ring of Gyges. I thought that I could see some of the men leering at the thought of actually possessing one. Some of the women seemed to be less enthusiastic about the whole prospect. To my question of whether they would buy such a ring, an idealist answered that she would—she could then do good with it. Others answered that they would use it only if they or their friends had been wronged. Still others wondered how many rings I had in stock. They suggested that perhaps I should require a license before others besides themselves could purchase one. They were too polite to wonder aloud about whether they would be able to trust me, the owner of so much power.

The experiment seems to prove the Sophist's point. For this purpose, it will serve to show very clearly how the fundamental assumptions we all make about human nature have great influence over the way in which we weigh opposing arguments. If we are as cynical as the Sophist, then we will think that the Sophist is the obvious winner of the debate. If we have a religious view of human nature, we will hold out for the possibility that a person will still honor justice even if he possesses a ring of Gyges.

Ch. 6 The View of the Sophist

JUSTICE AS AN ART

Warming to his role, Glaucon drives on, giving us deeper insight into the notion of justice as a useful good. Developing the favorite Greek notion that justice is some kind of an art, Glaucon brands temple robbers, ordinary thieves, and the like as definitely having no art. While these criminals are certainly egotists, they just as certainly are not enlightened. They are just small timers who have neither the imagination nor the guts to live life on a grand scale.

The real artists are those who break the law without getting caught. These are the people who go to the right schools, make the proper connections in society, and move in the most respectable circles. It takes great training, discipline, and connections not to get caught. But if people perfect the right skills, they may become rich by using their skills in law or politics and then win an award for public service.

In short, for one to be a master at practicing justice as a useful good, one must be adept at maintaining the appearance of justice. For it is only the right appearance that will provide the proper invisibility for the enlightened to work their will. Even then, such people might get caught. But if they have had the foresight to make the right connections, they may survive with less damage to their reputations.

In short, the Sophist is saying that people have no choice about being egotists because that quality arises from their very nature. The thing that people do have a choice about is whether they will be enlightened or unenlightened egotists. Mother Theresa, for example, would be considered an enlightened egotist because she was respected by the whole world. Conversely, Hitler would be considered an unenlightened egotist because his name today is taken for the very title of

Ch. 6 The View of the Sophist

evil itself. If he had won the war, perhaps things might have been different. But he lost, thus committing the only sin possible in this scheme of things. For the really enlightened never lose, never get caught!

A LOGICAL CONNECTION

We now see that there is a logical connection between justice considered as useful and justice considered as a mere appearance. If the only motive for being just is fear, what happens when there is no fear of getting caught? What happens when one, having gotten used to the game, learns how to get around the law? Is there any reason in this case for not cultivating merely the appearance of justice?

The pursuit of justice as a useful good turns into the pursuit of the mere appearance of justice. A person wanting absolute liberty will find the mere appearance to be quite useful because everyone else also wants absolute liberty and so will not take too kindly to those who are known to be exactly like themselves. Therefore, everyone has to learn how to use the appearances of justice in order to do what they wish, even to practice the greatest injustice if they desire to do so.

At this point, there is no great mystery to the sinister aspect of pursuing justice as a useful good. To those brought up with a conscience, it is an evil pursuit. But to those who conceive the highest goal of human nature to be absolute freedom, it is the only logical path to follow. To those who hold that human existence is simply the survival of the fittest, it is the only realistic or sane philosophy to follow.

JUSTICE AS AN INTRINSIC GOOD

Having polished to a fine finish his account of justice as a useful good, the Sophist then proceeds to fashion another account—that of justice as an intrinsic good.

Ch. 6 The View of the Sophist

He has, of course, been acquainted with people who make a profession of pursuing this higher notion of justice. In fact, those following the religious tradition will make this profession. But the Sophist views these people as either simple-minded or hypocritical. The simple-minded are the sincere practitioners of virtue who refuse to face the grim facts about the realities of life, particularly political life. The hypocritical are those who have learned how, to turn their profession of virtue into a kind of Ring of Gyges—their profession being a front which renders their real wickedness invisible.

The Sophist despises both types, but perhaps he detests the sincere more than the hypocritical. For he is really in basic sympathy with the latter, who is very much like himself. The only difference between them is their attitude towards religion. The Sophist fights it while the hypocrite uses it. But he has no sympathy or understanding of the sincere, who stand opposed to him in the most radical manner, who stand as his greatest and most determined opponents. For the Sophist holds that the highest goal of man is to exercise perfect liberty, the greatest evil being the total loss of this liberty. The sincere practitioner of virtue, on the other hand, maintains not only that human beings should never murder, steal, or cheat but also that they should choose death rather than dishonoring themselves by these deeds. The religious person, therefore, being the most opposed to the perfect freedom desired by the Sophist, is his greatest enemy.

A TEST

The Sophist, drawing upon his talents as a cynic, states that if the just person loves justice for its own sake, then let him have it, but without any good consequences that might flow from it. Thus, the Sophist reasons with relish that if the just person is blinded, scourged, and finally impaled, that person

Ch. 6 The View of the Sophist

should still be happy because, though he does not have the good consequences that ordinarily flow from practicing justice, he still has his justice. Let virtue be its own reward!

The Sophist feels that in making this demand he is only being reasonable. He cannot really tell, he will insist, whether a Socrates practices justice simply for its own sake or only for the sake of its consequences. To appease the suspicions of this cynic, therefore, the defender will have to show how the just person will be a lover of justice itself.

The Sophist is arguing with Socrates in the same way the Devil argued with God in the story of Job. The Devil claimed that Job was not faithful because God was worthy in Himself of such devotion, but only because God had showered so many blessings upon him. In other words, he claimed that Job was faithful only because of the good things it brought him. But let me put some trials on him, says the Devil, and then we'll see how faithful he is! In other words, the Devil will put curses rather than blessings upon Job in order to see whether the man will still honor God. The Devil feels that he has an open-and-shut case if God should ever agree to his demands. For the Devil, like the Sophist, figures that everyone else is just like himself, meaning that they will be good when they can get something out of it.

ADEIMANTUS PRESENTS HIS POINT

Now, Adeimantus, the older brother of Glaucon, jumps in to make the question even tougher for Socrates. He forbids Socrates to defend his notion of justice in the same way that parents, poets, and priests often do.[19] They often recommend the practice of justice to their young charges by dwelling upon the rewards of such practice. For example, parents will urge their children

---

[19] See sections 364 367.

Ch. 6 The View of the Sophist

on with such sentiments as honesty being the best policy. Teachers will proclaim that if the student is virtuous, they will also be a worldly success. Poets and priests will recommend the pursuit of virtue and the avoidance of vice by portraying vividly the heavenly rewards that will come to the virtuous and the hellish punishments that will come to the vicious. Adeimantus considers that all such appeals for justice are simply different ways of turning justice merely into a useful good. He therefore lays down the condition that Socrates cannot make any appeal to the rewards and punishment of an afterlife in defense of his notion of justice. The champion must be restricted to defending the position that justice should be pursued simply for its own sake.

Having set this final condition, the two young men rest their case. As if to distance themselves from the cynical role they have assumed, they then speak to Socrates from their own hearts. They want to hear from him a defense of justice as a quality to be valued simply for its own sake. Health is valued in this way. Even if no other benefit came, health would still be a valuable thing in itself because it directly perfects the body. Knowledge is also valued in this way. Even if no other benefit came, knowledge would still be a valuable thing in itself because it directly perfects the intellect. The young men figure that if justice is an intrinsic good, it must somehow perfect the soul, independently of whether other men or even the gods know about it.

AN INTRINSIC GOOD

Their conviction that justice is an intrinsic good explains the way they have developed the argument of the Sophist. They have drawn an absolute contrast between useful and intrinsic good. The former have no value in themselves but are sought only for

Ch. 6 The View of the Sophist

the sake of their consequences. The latter are sought only because they have value in themselves and not for any consequences they might bring. Thus, the really good man is to have a bad reputation while the really evil man is to have a good one. The really good man is to be a loser in this life while the really evil man is to be a winner.

All of the conditions laid down by the young men point to one thing. If Socrates is to defend the notion of justice as intrinsic, he must do so within the time frame of birth and death. In other words, he is restricted to appealing to the evidence supplied by human life as lived on this earth. And when he does use this evidence, he cannot cite worldly success as a motive for pursuing justice; he can only cite as evidence the effect that this quality called justice has upon the soul or the innermost heart of the person possessing it. For if justice is an intrinsic good, it must be good no matter how it appears to other men or even to the gods.

PLATO, THE PHILOSOPHICAL ARTIST

From the above we can see Plato at work as both the philosopher and the dramatic artist. As a philosopher, he is very precise about the exact notion of justice that he wishes to depict. This very precision makes for a very dramatic beginning to the contest. At first glance, it seems as if the Sophist has won the game before it has even started if we were to judge the matter in the way that people ordinarily do. It seems to put Socrates at a very severe disadvantage. For the views of the Sophist seem to be those of most, or at least of many, of the people who have made history. The reader then has a two-fold treat in front of him. There is the curiosity of seeing how Socrates can win the game after seemingly granting to the enemy all the points he needs. And there is the intellectual spectacle of watching a great philosopher erect a philosophical justification for virtue or justice.

Ch. 6 The View of the Sophist

THE INFLUENCE OF MODERN POLITICAL SCIENCE

Added to the influence that the cynical spirit has always had on people trying to judge human affairs, there is also the influence that modern political science has had on us for the last four hundred years. Modern political thought begins where the influence of classical political thought ends; namely, at the period in which Machiavelli disposes of Plato, Aristotle, and the Gospels in favor of his own views. He mocks the ancients for talking about what individuals and rulers *should do* and suggests that people study the way in which people actually behave. In this way, the true ruler will give up an idealism that distracts him from political reality to gain a realism that prepares him for decisive action.

The basic elements that are found in the views of the Sophist have become the staples of modern political science. Both assume that human beings are, by nature, egotists whose highest good is perfect liberty or freedom. This means that people are, by their very nature, only out for themselves. This renders the relationship between these individuals conflictual or competitive. In other words, society or the community is a mere collection of super-energized atoms, all charging about either in collision or collusion for the sake of trying to come out on top. In this struggle, there is no such thing as Truth or Right; there is only Might. In other words, might makes right. Sheer power is the ultimate creator of justice.

CHAPTER SEVEN

SOCRATES BEGINS HIS ANSWER

INTRODUCTION

In this chapter, we will observe how Socrates begins his answer to the challenge posed by Glaucon speaking for the Sophist. The first thing we wish to note is that Socrates begins his answer in the way a professor would; he begins at the beginning, the logical point from which a philosophical explanation should start. Now, I have nothing against professors as such, being one myself. Nor do I have any great reluctance about reading an explanation that begins at the beginning. Indeed, I am grateful when thinkers extend this courtesy to me. The only trouble with such a start is that it is dull. Straight philosophy is often a rather pedestrian affair. Poetry, drama, and satire are much more exciting. And so I wonder why Plato, who certainly knows how to hold the interest of readers, allows his hero to make such a dull beginning in the face of such a lively challenge.

I think the answer is that Plato is addressing a listener like Glaucon who, though deluged by all the resources of a corrupt culture that knows how to attract attention to itself, is still not swept away. This special type of listener has already seen through the seductive appearance of worldliness. In his personal life, he has already made up his mind to take up a life that might have appeared to him in his wilder days as too sober and dull. We know this from the fact that he is a companion of a man like Socrates. In his intellectual life, he is now ready to do whatever it takes to answer the Sophist. And

Ch. 7 Socrates Begins His Answer

what it takes, in this case, is a great deal of philosophical thinking in the classical 'tradition,' which involves a lot of hard and undramatic work. For a person like Glaucon, then, the beginning of the account by Socrates is quite appropriate—it begins at the beginning.

WHAT IS THIS BEGINNING?

What is this beginning? Socrates announces that before attempting to define the nature of justice, he will examine the nature of human community. He will proceed in this way because it is only in the human community that just and unjust actions are found. In other words, only human beings act justly or unjustly. This point is so obvious that the reader may wonder why I even bother to mention it. But the whole point of explaining something philosophically is to make obvious things explicit for the simple reason that people often overlook or forget them in their haste to form a theory to their own liking. As philosophers, Socrates and Plato are well aware of their obligation to make contending parties look to the fundamentals as a way of settling disputes.

THE CONFLICTUAL COMMUNITY

The Sophist did not mistakenly overlook these fundamentals. He first considered the community before defining justice. He saw the human community as conflictual or competitive in nature and so defined justice as a useful good. He supplied the framework or context in which his notion of justice made sense.

THE COOPERATIVE COMMUNITY

We will now see how Socrates, after describing the human community as essentially cooperative or organic in nature,

Ch. 7 Socrates Begins His Answer

will define justice as an intrinsic good. At this point of the argument, the basic question for the reader is whether the human community is essentially conflictual or cooperative. That is the key point around which the basic question about the nature of justice turns.

AN ANALOGY[20]

The very first thing that Socrates does is to compare the search for the nature of justice to the project of learning how to read. If a person wishes to learn, he would be fortunate if he could first practice on a text with large letters before proceeding to the same text written in smaller letters. Similarly, if a group of inquirers is looking for the definition of the just and the unjust, they look for it in the community before proceeding to look for it in the individual. The community is the individual written in large letters.

---

[20] See section 368d.

A REASONABLE APPROACH

This approach seems reasonable, because the entities that are just or unjust are human actions caused by individuals living in a community. Hence, if one wishes to understand the notions of justice and injustice, one should first understand the community in which people relate to one another. But do all inquirers share the same notion of human community? Probably not. Therefore, Socrates suggests that everyone should put their heads together to build up the notion of community, step-by-step. People will then become more aware of the views they actually hold instead of taking them for granted in an unreflecting way.

THE COMMUNITY ACCORDING TO THE SOPHIST

In giving his account of the origin and nature of justice, the Sophist first builds up

Ch. 7 Socrates Begins His Answer

his notion of the human community. It consists of individual human beings, who, by their very nature, take their highest good to be the exercise of perfect liberty. Such a community must, of its very nature, be conflictual and competitive. For if everyone considers it their natural right to be perfectly free, they will have to compete with each other. People living together cannot possibly act entirely as they wish. Here, we have a picture of the human community as an arena in which individuals battle or compete with one another. We also have a picture of the nature of a human being: one whose greatest right and highest goal is to be absolutely free. In other words, we have the view that the human being is, by nature, an egotist. Only an egotist can take, as a working principle of his life, that he be able to do whatever he wants with impunity.

JUSTICE IN THE CONFLICTUAL COMMUNITY

At this point, there is no such thing as justice in this state of the natural man. But the conflicts engendered by this natural state prompt the majority of human beings to fashion or invent the notion of justice in order to mitigate the conflict. They strike a bargain or make a contract whereby they will give up their right to perfect liberty to avoid total slavery. The government will embody this contract and see to it that people abide by its conditions.

We now have a new picture of the human individual. The majority will have to obey because they will have neither the power nor the imagination to do otherwise. The minority, however, will be able to escape these conditions because it will have discovered its own form of the Ring of Gyges. In brief, we will have the supermen and the slobs, the masters and the slaves.

Ch. 7 Socrates Begins His Answer

We can see how the notion of the Human City as a competitive arena and the nature of the individual as a perfect egotist supplies the contest in which justice is defined as a useful good. In his procedure, the Sophist has followed the general approach explained by Socrates. He has certainly not done this because Socrates has recommended it but because one cannot possibly give a fundamental account of a notion like justice unless one takes into account the nature of the human being in both his communal and individual aspects. In proceeding in this way, therefore, the Sophist is simply being intelligent.

THE SOCRATIC NOTION OF COMMUNITY

Let us now observe how Socrates goes about building up the notion of the human community to reveal the context in which intrinsic justice will function. Socrates first makes the generalization that the Human City comes to exist because no individual human being is self-sufficient. This brief statement says all that has to be said about his notion of the Human City. It means that individuals need partners or helpers to meet, among other things, their physical needs. In the areas of food, drink, and shelter, individuals specialize in their work instead of trying to do everything for themselves. They become farmers, weavers, carpenters, and toolmakers, providing not only or even primarily for themselves, but for others. They must consequently exchange their products or services for the things they do not have. The end result is the formation of the Human City, which must inculcate the virtue of cooperation among its members in order to function properly.

Ch. 7 Socrates Begins His Answer

JUSTICE IN THE SOCRATIC COMMUNITY

This Human City is an organism in which the units cooperate rather than an arena in which the units compete. In an organic community, the just thing will be any deed that promotes harmony. The wrong or unjust thing will be any deed that disrupts this harmony (If, on the other hand, the nature of the Human City is an arena in which egos compete with each other for dominance, the right or just thing will be any deed that effectively promotes total freedom while the wrong thing will be any deed that limits it.)

THE THREE PARTS OF THE SOCRATIC HUMAN CITY

For the rest of Book Two and all of Book Three, Socrates continues to build up, in theory, the rest of the Human City until it can be seen as a whole divided into three parts.

There are the Rulers, the Guardians, and the Workers.[21] Why these three parts? In any type of human community, there must be people who guide the community, people who protect it from internal and external enemies, and people who provide it with the necessities of life.

In the next chapter, we'll analyze Book Four where Socrates describes how these parts function in a cooperative rather than in a competitive way. But right now, lets examine a major implication about the nature of man to be found in this description of the community as cooperative in nature.

THE NATURE OF MAN

The implication is that man has the power of free choice. Why is this implied in Socrates' argument? Because the fact that

---

[21] This final category includes, as well, the rest of humanity; e.g., the old, the young, or the very ill.

Ch. 7 Socrates Begins His Answer

people band together to meet their needs in a cooperative way does not happen of necessity. Men can also enslave, kill, manipulate, trick, and lie to each other. The implication, then, is that man, of his very nature, has the possibility of forming either an organic or a competitive community, depending on how he chooses to exercise his free will. Before man makes these choices, he is neither just nor unjust, neither good nor evil. He acquires these qualities by the choices he makes in life.

The Sophist has a different notion of free choice. To him, the human being is necessarily one whose highest goal is the attainment of perfect freedom and, therefore, one for whom the prosperity of another is always threatening or diminishing. As it is the nature of birds to fly and fish to swim, so, reasons the Sophist, is it the nature of man to be an egotist. Within this necessity there will be choice, but it will be the choice of being either an enlightened or an unenlightened egotist. A good or just deed will be an act, which primarily benefits the agent's interest, while an evil or unjust deed will be an act, which primarily violates his self-interest.

THE NATURE OF THE HUMAN CITY

The fact that Socrates and the Sophist have such a contrasting view of the nature of man shows us why there are difficulties about expressions such as "the nature of the Human City" or "the nature of community." To the Sophist, these expressions mean the way human communities actually are. To prove his case, he points to the history of mankind, citing century after century in which men related to each other as masters and slaves or as wolves with wolves. Like Machiavelli and other founders of modern political science, he considers that the only choice open to men is whether they will be winners or losers, crafty or naive, enlightened or unenlightened.

Ch. 7 Socrates Begins His Answer

But when Socrates and Plato (and the rest in the classical tradition) speak of the nature of the Human City, they are speaking of the way it *should* be. They are saying that communities *should* be organic or cooperative, not necessarily that all communities are that way. They take this view because they hold that man has the power to choose his path to happiness. If he makes the right choices, he will attain his goal. This means that man in community *should* choose to cooperate rather than compete. To speak of the nature of the Human City as cooperative or organic, then, is to state the ideal that man should strive for the goal that will fulfill the possibilities of his human nature.

WHEN SOPHISTS AND SOCRATICS MEET

The reader can now see why there is so much confusion when Sophists and Socratics use the term "the nature of man" or "the nature of the Human City." The Sophist is referring to the way most men behave and become very impatient when classical thinkers talk about human nature as an ideal that people should live up to. The classical thinker, on the other hand, is viewing man as a creature with two paths open to him. The first represents the way in which he will be happy, thus fulfilling the design of his nature. The second represents the way in which he will be miserable, thus departing from the design of his nature.

NO NEED TO PUSH FURTHER

There is no need now to push any further in our analysis of the argument of Socrates. For now, it's enough to show that unlike the Sophist, Socrates has determined that the Human City should be cooperative or organic in structure and, in so doing, has sent his argument down a path which diverges radically from that of the Sophist. We will

Ch. 7 Socrates Begins His Answer

pursue the rest of the argument in the next chapter. For the rest of this chapter, we will try to bring home how important it is to have a sound notion of the nature of the human community to erect a philosophical defense of the traditional view of morality.

A MODERN EXAMPLE

Perhaps the reader has already noticed the similarity between the views of the Sophist and those expressed by many Americans today on the question of sexual morality. The Sophist holds for as much freedom as the individual can attain for himself. Many modern Americans feel the same way in the area of sexuality; they feel that they should be perfectly free to do as they please without anyone else imposing their views on them. Thus, many women insist that it their right and theirs alone to decide whether they shall have an abortion or not. Teenagers and college students insist that how they behave sexually is nobody else's business but their own. Homosexuals and lesbians mount protests against the Catholic Church for condemning what they consider to be the legitimate exercise of their sexual preferences. And a great many married couples, Catholics included, insist that contraception is not only a right but even a duty for responsible parents. Psychologists maintain that masturbation among the young is but a stage in their natural sexual development.

All of these views, in one way or another, consider the realm of sexuality to be a purely private one which the individual alone has the right to regulate.

HOW DOES PLATO ANSWER?

Plato is not a model of good sense in this area. In fact, he is practically insane on the subject of human sexuality Though he is correct in maintaining the organic view of

Ch. 7 Socrates Begins His Answer

community, he is incorrect in his determination of its basic unit. He says that the basic unit is the individual who, in his role as specialist in his work, must cooperate with others as they must cooperate with him. He does not, like his pupil Aristotle, make the male and the female, the husband and the wife the basic unit of the human community. He tries to erect a Human City in which the basic unit is not a couple but an individual specialist. In this matter, he turns out to be perhaps a greater revolutionary in sexual morality than even the Sophists, ancient or modern.

A NEW SEXUAL ETHIC

In trying to displace the family as the foundation unit of society, Plato is instituting a whole new sexual ethic. In essence, Plato opts for the community of mates and of children. In other words, each individual will have many mates, and each child will have many mothers and fathers, and hundreds of brothers and sisters. The community of adults will allow an equality of roles between men and women, for, in all public matters, no account will be taken of their sexual differences. Women will not be regarded as potential mothers but will be treated as their talents warrant.

How then will the propagation of the race be handled? Certainly not by the family, regarded by Plato as a very poor institution for this purpose. Instead, the state will use all the best methods of breeding to ensure that a superior race is formed. This race will be raised and educated by professional child-care specialists.

NOT AN ANSWER

Plato's views are not an answer to the view of sexuality taken by the Sophists (and the modern Americans). If one wishes to make the structure of virtue intelligible, one

Ch. 7 Socrates Begins His Answer

will have to begin one's consideration, not just with the community as an organic structure, but with a community whose basic unit is the family. Once one has a clear idea of the family in mind, an idea which delineates the roles of husband and wife, father and mother, parents, and children, one will have the key to understanding the logic behind all the traditional sexual norms. But without this clear idea of the family, one may easily fall into the terrible mistake of viewing all norms of morality as impositions upon one's freedom. Without this clear idea of the importance of the family, one will more easily fall prey to the notion that the government and the rest of society are all threats to one's freedom. One will then attempt to throw off all notions of any discipline and restraint, acts which will make the individual more enslaved to his own passions and more vulnerable to the impositions of tyranny. For to give up the family and all the discipline it entails is simply to put out the welcome mat for the tyrant, either singular or collective.

ANOTHER SOLUTION

We now have a dilemma new to this book. The view of the Sophist in regard to sexual ethics seems to be wrong and yet Plato has not advanced a convincing answer.

But there is another view that takes into consideration the fact that sexual activity is not simply a private affair and poses the best response to the Sophist in this case.

THE JUDEO-CHRISTIAN TRADITION

The whole of this traditional moral code has no object other than the preservation of the family. And the family as inherited from the Judeo-Christian code demands that the exercise of sexuality be restricted entirely within the confines of marriage. Now this, of course, is a very high ideal for any society to

Ch. 7 Socrates Begins His Answer

achieve. For human beings show a decided weakness for exercising their sexuality in every state but the married one. They also show a weakness for separating the exercise of sexuality from the activity of reproduction. Thus, the whole of Christian sexual ethics can be understood as an elaborate set of norms whose aim is to promote marriage and to discourage its opposites because the health of the whole society depends upon the maintenance of the family.

Sexuality is not a private affair. It has the most public of effects—the creation of human beings. Without their coming into being, the human community simply has no future. The very existence of society then depends upon the sexual activity of individuals. If one wishes to have a realistic idea of the place of sexual activity in human affairs, one should think of it in terms of harnessing all the forces of society for the generation, maintenance, and education of its future. Americans in the 2020s have a much more vivid appreciation of this fact than did Americans in the 1960s. Then, we talked about the Sexual Revolution as if it were simply another form of recreation. Now, we see how the devastating effects of the revolution are all around us in the form of divorce, teenage pregnancy, AIDS, and a host of other social ailments.

TRADITIONAL MORALITY VERSUS SOPHISM

In paying attention to the full ramifications of human sexuality, we have simply been looking at the community as a cooperative organism rather than as a conflictual arena. One looks at the community as a conflictual arena when he considers sexuality a purely private affair in which he should have total freedom. This attitude will necessarily put him in conflict with others, who will necessarily be affected by the effects of his activity in this area. On the other hand,

Ch. 7 Socrates Begins His Answer

one looks at the community as a cooperative matter when one accepts responsibility for sexual activity, not as limitations upon his freedom, but a way of benefiting both the individual and the community. In a cooperative venture, to ensure the future of a society, its members will insist on self-discipline, deferred enjoyment, service, loyalty, and self-sacrifice. In other words, it will insist on all the qualities that make for sound and healthy families.

We see then that the ancient way of posing the two different ways in which one can consider the Human City are as relevant today as they were then. Sooner or later, a society will have to look at this whole matter in a saner way. At that point, it might be ready to pay attention to those who all along have been speaking good sense.

CONCLUSION

We have seen how central to the whole project of defining justice as an intrinsic good is to the effort of Socrates to start our inquiry with the notion of the community as cooperative or organic in nature. We have not yet seen precisely how a cooperative notion of community implies an intrinsic notion of virtue. But we have seen how it differs from the view of the community as a competitive arena, which generates the notion of justice as useful. That will be enough for this chapter.

We have also illustrated the vast difference it makes in contemporary discussions about sexual morality whether one starts with a notion of community that is based upon attaining total freedom (and is therefore necessarily conflictual) or with a notion of community that is cooperative, not as individual specialists, but as family units cooperating with other families to form the

Ch. 7 Socrates Begins His Answer

other institutions of society. Those filled with the heady drink of sexual liberation will not wish to hear any analysis like this but will instead accuse us of being fascists. But those trying to defend philosophically the traditional notions of morality will know how and where to start their considerations. It will be with a consideration of the nature of human community. On that all other considerations depend.

CHAPTER EIGHT

THE FINAL DEFINITION OF JUSTICE AS AN INTRINSIC GOOD

INTRODUCTION

In the previous chapter, it was established that the Human City, according to Socrates, should be organic and cooperative. The parts that must cooperate, we discovered, are three in number and consist of Rulers, Guardians, and Workers. In this chapter, we will see how Plato defines the virtues that these parts must have to succeed. These virtues (wisdom, courage, and moderation) will work together to create the crown of Plato's final argument:

the definition of justice itself. For clarity, it is worthwhile to summarize the stages of the argument before we get to this definition.

THE FOUNDATION

To quickly review, the foundation of Plato's argument consists of laying down the common ground, which all inquirers must have if they are to be fellow laborers. This ground has both an experiential and a philosophical level. On the experiential level, the inquirers accept the views of men like Cephalus and Glaucon, who already know in a practical way that justice is an intrinsic good. On the philosophical level, they accept the principle that will guide their inquiry, namely, that happiness is the objective standard by which the validity of any moral position is established.

Ch. 8 The Final Definition of Justice

THE MIDDLE STAGE

In the middle stage of the argument, the inquirers, having intellectually assembled the Human City piece by piece throughout Books Two and Three, are now philosophically certain that they have before them a city which is good. Before they started this assembling process, they already knew as a matter of experience that a cooperative is better than a competitive city. But now they all through the cooperation of its parts. They have examined their experiential knowledge in the light of the basic principle and arrived at the philosophical judgment that it is better than a competitive community.

THE VIRTUES

The next task of the inquirers is to discover exactly how the virtues fit into the cooperative enterprise that is a city. They already know in a vague way that they fit in.

They also know from experience with their religious and literary traditions that there are four main virtues: wisdom, courage, moderation, and justice.[22] But they do not as yet have any philosophical knowledge of why these virtues are good. To know why, they will have to see how each of these virtues in their particular way leads the community to happiness. And to know that, they will have to see how each of these virtues fits into the structure of an organic community. And to know that, they will have to see how each of the virtues fits into the proper part of the community.

The whole rhythm of this process of inquiry may be summarized as follows. Initially the inquirers grasp in a general way that a cooperative community leads to happiness. Subsequently, they deepen their grasp of what is involved in such a community and so acquire a more specific idea of its

---

[22] See section 427e.

Ch. 8 The Final Definition of Justice

connection with the attainment of happiness. In brief, the inquirers first accept with certitude the truth of a general outline of the matter and then proceed very carefully to fill in its details so that certitude is not lost.

VIRTUE NECESSARY TO THE RULERS

What is the quality most necessary to the rulers of a community if they are to maintain the organic nature of the Human City? Many might be inclined to say that it is the power to enforce their will. There is some truth here. But the possession of power cannot be enough. By itself, it is blind and requires direction. It is human knowledge that supplies this direction. The Sophist's Ruler uses his knowledge to direct power for his own benefit. The skill needed here is cunning or craft. On the other hand, the direction taken by the Rulers of the Socratic community is the promotion and preservation of its cooperative nature. Here, the

Ruler is directing all his knowledge toward the betterment of others. The goal of his employment of power is just the opposite of that of the Sophist.

Here, the knowledge of the Ruler is called wisdom. It is related to the skill of ship builders. Shoemakers, and farmers. For just as the workers know how to attain the end of their crafts, so the Ruler knows how to direct the community so that the final goal of happiness is attained. Yet, as we saw earlier, wisdom is unlike the technical arts. A man can be a great ship builder and yet have the soul of a thief. A man cannot be a wise ruler without having a great soul. Without that soul, he will not be able to persevere in using his intelligence and power for the sake of others. Hence, wise rulers must have clear intellects and steadfast hearts. Aristotle calls this type of wisdom *prudence,* which has both an intellectual and a moral component. The moral component fixes the heart of the Ruler on a love and devotion to the proper goal, warding off the seductions exerted by money, pleasure, honor, and pride. The intellectual component determines the right means to attain the goal. The result is that the community has a shape or a line as intelligible as that of a great ship wrought by a master builder. For reason has molded many individuals into an organic whole, a Human City. The prudence of the Ruler is not the calculating skill had by small souls. It is the great virtue, which puts a human stamp upon the community.

NO GREAT MYSTERY

The truth that rulers should be wise is no great mystery. It is a platitude that rulers should rule for the sake of the ruled. This truth, coming from the mouth of an orator, will almost certainly bore any audience. But this truth embodied in the actual behavior of any authority is far from boring. Everyone has had experience with authority in one of its various forms. Perhaps, in some few instances, one has had the experience of an authority using its considerable power for the advancement of those under it. One may recall the amazement and gratitude one felt when actually meeting an authority like this. One may also recall times in which authority merely used subordinates for its own purposes. In that context, any exhortation to working for the team or the group was often received with great cynicism, an entirely appropriate reaction.

Here, I have been appealing to the experience of the reader as evidence for the proposition that rulers should be wise. Decent people will take this evidence as being self-evident, meaning that one has simply to hear it in order to accept it. But, as I will never tire of repeating, a philosophical argument is more than this type of appeal. It consists in showing why Rulers should be wise. And this why is to be discovered by relating the particular virtue in question (wisdom) to the

Ch. 8 The Final Definition of Justice

right part (the Ruler) in the right type of community (organic) organized on the right ultimate principle (the attainment of happiness).

NOT TAKEN FOR GRANTED TODAY

Yet, in many intellectual circles today, the truths enunciated above are not accepted. How can that be? There are many different causes, but surely one of them is the fact that modern political science has been shaped by thinkers who based their thought on a denial of the principles outlined above. Men like Machiavelli and Hobbes scorned as unrealistic idealism the notion that Rulers should rule for the sake of the ruled. They figured that if rulers became concerned with doing the right thing according to reason, they would not be rulers for very long. They certainly had a point here. As history shows, the game of politics always seems to have favored the ruthless and unscrupulous. These thinkers, therefore, determined to put political philosophy on a new footing. Instead of talking about what rulers *should* do to further the common good, they would talk about what a ruler *must* do to survive at any cost. Hence, these thinkers share an uncanny resemblance to the Sophist. And it is this influence that permeates the thinking of political experts today. They instruct the candidate in the art of appearing to be concerned with the good of the community, maintaining that the one with the best appearance wins. They would never dream that any intelligent person might take the appearance seriously.

THE NEXT PART AND ITS CHARACTERISTIC VIRTUE

The next part of the Human City that Socrates considers is the guardian or soldier. It is not hard to identify the virtue that soldiers need to do their share in keeping the

Ch. 8 The Final Definition of Justice

community a cooperative or harmonious whole. It is courage. This is not simply the quality that makes the soldier formidable in battle. Pirates and brigands can be as fearless as lions and yet not be courageous in the estimation of Socrates. Courage is the virtue of fearing the right things. And the right things to fear are not death or the loss of pleasure or wealth. Instead, they are dishonor and cowardice. Thus, a soldier should fear the temptation of using his power to exploit his own people for the sake of acquiring wealth and pleasure. He should fear using his power as the shepherd Gyges used his ring. A soldier should also fear to flee from the enemy of his people to save his own life. His duty is to risk his own life even when the people he is protecting do not always respect him.

It is this notion of courage that shows upon it the imprint of wise rulers. They realize that training an army that will be ferocious towards enemies and yet tender towards the weak (the fellow citizens they have sworn to protect) is a very difficult task. Soldiers who are too tender may not be tough enough. And soldiers who are tough enough may be harsh or brutal. The Socratic definition of courage requires that it be reasonable. For only a reasonable training of the guardians will enable them to use their power in an appropriate way in widely different situations.

A little thought will show how powerful a boost to a cooperative community is the practice of the virtue of courage. What community cannot help but be deeply touched if its guardians actually risk their lives for its safety? Every time that a soldier or fire fighter or police officer risks his life, the bonds of the community are drawn tighter. Courage does have this simple but profound effect. When real courage is present in the guardians of a community, all of us assume that these members have pledged themselves to risk both their lives and the welfare of their families for the sake of the community.

Ch. 8 The Final Definition of Justice

When one thinks about it, it is surprising that people in a community take for granted that their guardians will be courageous. For courage is a very high virtue, demanding the sacrifice of one's life, a very high demand. Yet people take it for granted. Why? Perhaps one reason is that if the guardians of a community are not courageous, then that community will not last very long.

THE VIRTUE OF MODERATION, OR TEMPERANCE

The final part of the community that Socrates considers is the workers. Again, the virtue that Socrates attributes to that part is interesting. It is temperance or moderation. Since their function is to provide goods and services for both themselves and the whole community, they must moderate their own acquisitive tendencies to be able to benefit the whole. Just as in the individual, the appetites should be open to the rule of reason, so in the community, the people concerned directly with the material needs of the whole should be open to the direction of the rulers, who themselves are supposed to direct everything towards the common good. To put the point quite bluntly, those having direct power over the essential services of a community must not use that power to further their own interests, but to support the community. They need the virtue of temperance to attain this goal because, having real control over these services, they are able to hold the community hostage to their own personal welfare. Ordinary experience shows us that people who, perhaps, have never even consciously formulated for themselves the notion of virtue, nevertheless quickly recognize when some segment of the community is not doing the right thing. Even a thief who has been robbed will be quick to see the injustice of it all.

Ch. 8 The Final Definition of Justice

Wise	Courageous	Moderate	Just
Leaders	Guardians	Workers	Community

THE NATURE OF JUSTICE ITSELF

Having located the virtue proper to each part of the community, Socrates then looks for the nature of justice, the original goal of his inquiry. His conclusion is that justice is that quality residing in a community in which each of the parts performs its proper function. Justice, then, is that quality a community has when it functions, as the Human City should.

JUSTICE IN THE INDIVIDUAL

Having shown what justice looks like in the community, Socrates now turns his attention to the individual. It is obvious that the individuals who constitute this type of community already have a special character. Since each individual is either a Ruler, a Guardian, or a Worker, he already has a certain type of character as a member of a group. But the question remains: what qualities does the individual need to fulfill his role in the community? Furthermore, the individual has an independent existence apart from the community that a cell does not have apart from the organism. What, then, does justice as an intrinsic good look like in the individual?

Socrates divides the individual into the three parts possessed by any human being. These parts are what the scholars call Plato's tripartite division of the soul. When these parts of the individual each possess their proper virtue, then the individual is just. As we will soon see, the virtues, which perfect the three parts of the individual, have the

Ch. 8 The Final Definition of Justice

same name as those perfecting the three parts of the community.

THE RELATIONSHIP OF REASON TO THE EMOTIONS

Before seeing how Socrates argues his case, we should look back a moment to his view of human nature. In Book Three, Socrates goes to great lengths to discuss how the young should be educated. He stresses how the emotions of the young should be brought under the control of reason. Implicitly, then, he is saying that human beings are composed of reason and appetites, the latter being the source of the emotions or passions. The famous Platonic metaphor of the Chariot expresses this view of human nature. We have a chariot pulled by two great steeds and driven by a man. The man represents reason, which is supposed to direct. The two steeds represent the appetites, which are the forces of man's animal nature, which are to be directed. When reason grasps the truth and is successful in imprinting itself upon the appetites, there is harmony in the individual. When, however, any of the forces within man go out of control, the result is disharmony. Thus, if reason treats the appetites too harshly (not a very common fault) it kills the elemental forces in man. He is like a chariot being pulled around by two bunny rabbits. On the other hand, if reason does not deal firmly with the appetites (a much more typical failing), it is dominated by those forces. Man, then, is like a chariot pulled by two wild horses and driven by a ten-year-old. He is like an unguided missile charging about the heavens—a disaster waiting to happen.

GREAT EDUCATIONAL CONSEQUENCE

This view of the relationship between reason and the emotions has a great conse-

Ch. 8 The Final Definition of Justice

quence as far as education is concerned, a feature that Plato hammers out in many examples in Book Three. The priority that he gives to reason in his theory of virtue or justice leads him to give a large place to the emotions. For it is the emotions that are supposed to be imprinted by reason so that what a person knows to be right with his mind will be loved as beautiful by his heart. The true, the right, and the beautiful are one. The person who is really virtuous is the one who loves it. Consequently, when the ruler is leading the community or the educator instructing the young, both leaders pay a great deal of attention to the stories, songs, legends, dramas, buildings, statues and ceremonies which impress all of the senses. For these mold the feelings, which sway the heart, which often rules the head. These things embody notions about the nature of virtue. The leaders therefore cannot let the choice of such influential things be left to chance. Plato once said that he would gladly let his opponent have the powers of political office if he could be assured of determining the songs a people sings. We cannot say more on this important topic. But we should be aware that in his discussion of virtue Plato is not just a political philosopher or ethical thinker. He is also a poet and artist. All have a great bearing upon the formation of the good man.

HOW THE INDIVIDUAL IS COMPOSED OF AT LEAST TWO PARTS

To resume the argument: the first truth about the individual into which Socrates leads the group is about the division of man into reason and appetites. He proves that there is such a division by referring his audience to the common experience of knowing what one should do on the one hand but of being pulled to a more pleasant prospect on the other. All people have felt the pull between what reason dictates and what

Ch. 8 The Final Definition of Justice

feelings demand. For example, people on a lifeboat in the ocean certainly feel the desire to drink but refrain because they know that drinking salt water will kill them. Examples could be multiplied which illustrate the division all have felt between their head and heart, between their sense of duty and sense of pleasure. This tension Socrates takes as an indication of there being at least two parts in the individual: the rational and the appetitive.

TWO PARTS OF THE APPETITIVE

Socrates goes on to show how the appetites are divided into two types: the spirited appetite and the pleasure appetite. Here he lays down a view which was later developed by his pupil Aristotle and adopted by Aquinas over fifteen hundred years later. Ordinary experience shows that there is a similarity between human beings and animals. Both must have food, drink, and sex to survive individually and as a species. Thus, both have a natural drive towards these goods, a drive of the pleasure appetite. But there are difficulties both humans and animals have in acquiring these goods. Often, it is not easy to acquire these goods without expending great effort. Often, they must either fight or flee to protect themselves from others. Thus, there is also a natural drive in all animals, both rational and non-rational, to preserve themselves in difficult circumstances. This is the drive of the spirited appetite.

In human beings, these drives, passions, or emotions may or may not be open to the guidance of reason. If people are brought up well, the appetites are open to reason. Thus, when the spirited appetite takes on the guidance of reason, the human being pursues honor and self-preservation in a reasonable way. Also, when the pleasure appetite takes on the guidance of reason, the human being pursues the pleasurable goods in a reasonable way. The result is that the individual not only

Ch. 8 The Final Definition of Justice

has an intellectual conviction of what is right, but also a taste or desire for the right thing.

TEMPERATE

THREE VIRTUES FOR THREE PARTS

Seeing how Socrates divided the human being into three parts, we also see how easy it is for him to use the same three virtues here that he has already used in regard to the community. Thus, reason will be perfected by the virtue of wisdom, the spirited appetite by the virtue of courage, and the pleasure appetite by the virtue of temperance. In other words, the whole being of the individual will be imprinted by the mark of reason, which ensures that the person is a harmonious entity. Only in this harmonious entity does the virtue of justice reside. Justice in this case is but another name for a general quality denoting the three specific virtues perfecting each part.

A REVIEW

Having completed the outline for the Socratic argument urging that justice is an intrinsic good, let us sit back for a moment and review it. Going back to the conditions laid down by Glaucon and his brother, we recall that Socrates is forbidden to bring in any arguments about the afterlife to support his position. A related condition is that Socrates cannot appeal to any good earthly consequences that might come from the possession of justice. The point of these conditions is that, since Socrates has chosen to defend justice as an intrinsic good, he must defend it strictly on its own merits. He must show it to be valuable in itself. The possession

Ch. 8 The Final Definition of Justice

of virtue must be its own reward, independently of how other men or even the gods view it.[23] As a thing with a definite identity and reality of its own, it must be a reality in this life and, therefore, open to the view of those who are interested in seeking out the real.

CONCERNING THE CONDITIONS

Concerning the first condition, Socrates has confined his argument just to the experience of this life. He has appealed to the evidence supplied by human life both in its communal and its individual aspects. The argument, basically, is that, unless people have virtue, they will not be happy on this earth, either as communities or as individuals. For they will have dissonance, not harmony, within themselves and they will have conflict, not cooperation, in their

---

[23] See section 367d.

communities. Plato is, in effect, arguing that justice is not a luxury that human beings may or may not choose. It is a necessity, if human life is to be human. Here, he is not appealing to any particularly esoteric or ethereal motive for the practice of virtue. He is making an appeal to the understanding of all people, which pertains intimately to the lives of all people.

Concerning the second condition, Plato is arguing that justice is a habit or skill which is implanted in the human soul and becomes, as later thinkers say, second nature. There is no more intimate possession that the soul may have. Justice preserves the soul's harmony—it preserves the community. It is not some mere appearance put on for the sake of acquiring some external good. It colors the very way our minds and hearts work. It is the most significant perfection or completion that the soul can acquire. Therefore, it is worth something in itself. It is even more valuable than life itself. For to

Ch. 8 The Final Definition of Justice

preserve it, its possessors may be required to give up their lives as a witness to its goodness. Even in decadent ages, people will expect this of soldiers and of philosophers who annoy them, like Socrates.

Socrates has argued that there is an absolute and necessary connection between justice and happiness. If there is no wisdom, courage, or moderation there cannot possibly be any happiness or harmony. And if human beings do not acquire harmony or happiness by their efforts, then their efforts are a failure and so, too, are their lives.

MATERIAL SHAPED
BY THE DEFINING PROCESS

What happens when the ordinary experience of men like Cephalus and Glaucon—the stuff of proverbs, stories, and maxims—is shaped intellectually by the defining process? It gives the experience sharpness and precision. It explains exactly why the facts of moral experience are the way they are. The fundamental reason why the parts of the community should cooperate is because only then will harmony be attained. This harmony demands the presence of justice in the form of the three virtues in their respective parts. And the fundamental reason that reason should control appetite is because only then can the individual be happy. Thus, the individual must be just, must have the three virtues.

The precise shape given to the materials of experience have the same simplicity, universality, and fundamental nature in the philosophical order as the materials themselves have in the practical order of life. This common shape allows Plato to say that morality is fundamentally objective, the same for all human beings in all times and in all places. It permits him to claim that there are absolute norms of behavior, which cannot change with the times. It is possible for an experienced person who does not know

Ch. 8 The Final Definition of Justice

philosophy to make the same claims. And yet such a person (like Glaucon, for example) will not have the intellectual clarity to defend such claims against the arguments of others like the Sophists. Having gone through the process of definition, however, people like Glaucon acquire the intellectual sophistication to objectify their experience and defend their claims. Thus, the knowledge of the defining process does bring about a qualitative change in the intellect of decent people. It makes them less vulnerable to being seduced by the intellectual fashions of the day. They will be able to argue that moral norms are objective, not relative; that they are stable, not changing—this is the point of going through all the labor of mastering the steps of a long philosophical argument.

LOOKING AHEAD

The argument of Socrates is not yet finished. To meet the challenge laid down by

The Right Way to Live

Glaucon, the inquirers have to give their portrayal of justice as a useful good as a preparation of judging which notion of justice is the right one. We will follow this process in the next chapter.

CHAPTER NINE

PORTRAIT OF JUSTICE AS A USEFUL GOOD

INTRODUCTION

Back in Chapter Seven, we saw how Socrates, after listening to the challenge delivered with great fire and dash by Glaucon, settled down with his fellow inquirers to a long and sometimes tedious search for justice as an intrinsic good, a search we have just finished. Plato is enough of a literary craftsman not to leave his hero Socrates in the position of trying to win an argument just by answering with a long philosophical inquiry. Somehow, Plato must allow Socrates to add to his philosophical answer some fire and dash of his own.

What form will this counterattack take? We will get some idea of the answer by looking at the problem Socrates has to meet. In his speech, Glaucon depicts the Sophist as wise and experienced instead of as an evil person. The Sophist is praised as one who will use his Ring of Gyges to the best advantage. He is admired as one who has gone to the best schools, moved in the best circles, and made the right connections in high society. In contrast, Glaucon depicts men like Socrates as inexperienced fools instead of really good persons. In an even more cynical vein, he portrays them as liars for claiming not to use the Ring if they got the chance. For, according to the Sophist, it is the very nature of man to use that Ring if he ever gets his hands upon it!

The basic problem that Socrates has to meet, then, is that the discourse of the Sophist

Ch. 9 Portrait of Justice as a Useful Good

is aimed at the ears of the young, whether in years or in character. The youthful lack experience of life, and the young in character repeat the same experience over and over again, thereby showing an inability to learn. This deficiency in either not having, or in not learning from experience means that a person gets no benefit from the passage of time. Consequently, he will be taken in by the outward show that the rich and powerful are experts in projecting; he has not had enough experience of the world to see beneath the facade. He will also be taken in by experiences that purport to be happiness because of their ecstatic intensity. He will need time before he can see such experiences for what they often are—the mere thrill associated with being seduced by some glittering appearance as a prelude to the agony of being enslaved. He will need time before he can see that real happiness entails a degree of peace and contentment that he in his youth might have described as "being dead and not knowing it."

WHAT SOCRATES HAS TO DO

What Socrates has to do is to look at the human situation in the long term. Only the passage of time reveals the inner reality behind the outward appearances. Thus, Socrates will take the Sophist's account of justice and project it through time. Before he does this, he will briefly review his own notion of justice to serve as the ideal standard by which to judge any community or individual. Then, he will examine four different types of community, which deviate from this ideal.

The first one is based upon the pursuit of honor and does not look very evil. The second, which is derived from the first, is based upon the pursuit of riches, and appears to be neither as noble as the first nor as evil as the successors. The third, which is derived from the second, is based upon love of absolute liberty, in this case, the license to do and enjoy whatever one wishes. The last (and worst) is based upon love of the sick pleasures of life and results in the enslavement of all concerned, both rulers and subjects.

In this way, Socrates is attacking the Sophist in his own backyard. The Sophist claims to have hard-headed realism on his side. The aim of Socrates is to show that this "realism" is a fake by looking at events over a long period of time and seeing the way things really happen.

THE IDEAL STANDARD

Before proceeding to the deviations, let us briefly recall again the ideal standard of justice. It is fundamentally based upon the rule of right reason in both the community and the individual. As far as the community is concerned, this norm of reason means that wise rulers have a primary concern for objective truth. We will see more of what this involves in the next chapter. But for now it is enough to note that the practical effect of this concern for truth is that authorities rule the other parts of the community (the military and the business interests) for the sake of harmony in the whole. However, when the concern for truth lessens, either the military or the business interests will supplant the proper rulers, leaving the Human City in conflict. As far as the individual is concerned, this norm of reason requires the person direct his appetites so that he can maintain harmony within himself. When, however, either the spirited or the pleasure appetites slip out from under the rule of reason and themselves take the preeminent position, there will be personal disorder and unhappiness. At first the disorder on the communal and individual levels may not seem so dangerous, except perhaps to the experienced eye. But with the passage of time, Plato argues, it will be apparent to all because they will be its victims. Here, in a nutshell, is the thesis that Plato will expound with a wealth of detail.

Ch. 9 Portrait of Justice as a Useful Good

Let us now proceed to the first deviation from the ideal, the timocratic.

THE BIRTH OF TIMOCRACY

The term *timocrat* is derived from its Greek meaning: the rule of honor. Plato tells a little story illustrating how a son moves away from the ideals of his father and becomes a timocrat. There is a father who is representative of the ideal social order. After having spent many years honorably serving the community as a member of the ruling class, he now devotes much of his time to study and contemplation. He is not much interested in keeping up with the family's social status, either in the way of consuming conspicuously or of fighting in the law courts. The son admires his father, but at the same time is bombarded by complaints from his mother and the servants. They resent the seeming indifference of the master to the family honor. When the son grows up, he pays less attention to the cultivation of reason but is not swallowed up by a total concern for social and political advantages. Instead, he pursues honor in the way of a military man.

HONOR OVER REASON

This brief story has all the elements that mark the honor-seeking individual. In his single-minded pursuit of honor, he dethrones reason from its function of contemplating the truth and regulating the passions. The result is that, instead of pursuing the safety of both himself and the City in a reasonable way, he makes military power the absolute concern. The cultivation of honor, not wisdom, then becomes the goal. Reason is turned from being a master to being a servant. From its primary function of contemplating the truth, reason becomes a kind of technical advisor to help implement the design of ambition. All subjects of military science are held, of course, in high esteem while philosophy is put very low on the list. Even the passions of the pleasure appetite are repressed. Thus, there is a certain high-mindedness and discipline to be found in this type of individual. But there is also a certain amount of brutal insensitivity toward the self and others.

THE TIMOCRATIC COMMUNITY

In this type of community, the military have all the political power, thus subjugating both those with a concern for the common good and those with economic interests. Everything in the society is focused on maintaining military might as a means of keeping both subject populations and outsiders under control. There is much talk of honor and duty and the nation. But the high-minded talk masks brutal oppression for those not in the military caste.

Socrates goes into a great deal of detail describing this type of society. He had his experience of the Spartans to draw upon. But all that we moderns have to do in order to get the same insight is to read the newspapers and watch TV. On the political scene, we have but to observe what happens to America in its role as a world power. Military prowess becomes a very important thing, and defeat is taken very seriously. On the social scene, we have many examples of people who have given their all for success, be it in literature, art, music, or entertainment. On the foreign scene, we observe how military power dominates the affairs of most other nations.

Here, in a nutshell, is the summary of the elaborate account that Socrates gives of the first deviation from the ideal. Let us reflect upon it for a moment to see how it, though still a comparatively noble type, has all the seeds of disintegration within it.

Ch. 9 Portrait of Justice as a Useful Good

DEPARTING FROM REASON

In departing from the rule of reason to the rule of honor, the timocrat has all the basic characteristics of those who hold for justice as a merely useful good. Fortitude or courage is no longer the virtue which places the military under the guidance of the ruler or the spirited appetite at the service of reason. Instead, it becomes a value that people of a certain temperament may happen to consider as the highest priority of the Human City. This value is not what the needs of a sane community require. Rather, it is what the unrestrained drive or ego of powerful people choose to impose upon the community. This imposition of values, which are merely arbitrary instead of reasonable, will necessarily result in conflict between the parts of the community and eventually between the individuals themselves. This imposition of values will also lead to the cultivation of the appearance of virtue. A counterfeit fortitude and patriotism will be used to countenance a kind of villainy.

Socrates seems to be saying that while all these effects of timocracy are indeed present in this type of community, they are still in seed form. Perhaps for the sake of argument, he allows that a community like Sparta has a certain dignity despite all its shortcomings. Yet, in this community's flight from reason provides the seeds of further disintegration. In the next portrait, he shows how the honor seeker can give way to the moneygrubber, the oligarch.

BIRTH OF THE OLIGARCHY

Socrates goes on to depict the birth of the oligarch as a degeneration from the timocrat. A timocratic father, having devoted his whole life to military honor, falls into disgrace due to some defeat. As a result, the family hopes are wrecked. Experiencing this disaster, his son is disillusioned with ideals of glory and honor, which seem to be so ephemeral; he resolves that the acquisition of wealth is the only sure way to security. He forswears the pursuit of honor for that of money. In the soul of this individual, the goals of the pleasure appetite assume the throne. These goals are not those of a desire for luxuries but only for those items, which are absolutely necessary for the maintenance of life. This is the hard driving tycoon who has channeled his intelligence and his appetites to winning the war of economics. As he is described today, "he takes no prisoners."

THE OLIGARCHIC COMMUNITY

Here, the wealthy rather than the military assume political authority. Only citizens who have a certain amount of riches are qualified to take part in government. In educational policy, the mind becomes the servant of the acquisitive instincts. In the affairs of the nation, all the energy that formerly went into military dominance are turned toward commercial superiority.

In this type of rule, law is not used to further the interests of the common good, but of the wealthy. It furthers and preserves the distance between the wealthy and the poor. The community is two nations rather than one. Conflict between the two parts of the community is increased. Justice itself becomes a mere appearance by which one faction tries to maintain its dominance over the other. The threat of revolution lurks in the wings.

This type of society assumes much more the utilitarian model laid out by the Sophist in Chapter Six. The essence of the individual is enlightened self-interest and that of the community is sheer competition. It would be easy to imagine members of such a society extolling the merits of competition as the only way to preserve a proper standard of living and keep the Human City on its toes.

Ch. 9 Portrait of Justice as a Useful Good

THE BIRTH OF THE DEMOCRATIC COMMUNITY

The next story illustrates the formation of the democratic character. The hard-driving, oligarchic father produces a son who has all the advantages that wealth can bring without any of the pains in acquiring it. The son admires the father but does not relish the hard life that the serious pursuit of wealth demands. In this distaste, he is supported by his peers, who only think of ways to spend and enjoy money. Thus, his soul is torn between the ideal of hard work and the prospect of enjoying his wealth.

He is like many a college student in the 1960s who deplored the materialistic ways of his Cadillac-driving parents. He has liberated himself from those ways—he drives a Mercedes. Being a son of his father, he can still work very hard. But being a child of prosperity, he can also play very hard.

THE DEMOCRATIC SOCIETY

Political authority is assumed by the majority, whose slogan is freedom. Reason, honor, and wealth are all subjugated to the goal of everyone having a right to enjoy their liberty. Whereas in the two former regimes, there was a kind of discipline and purpose, there is not much discipline in the new regime. The many now have their chance to 'use" the law in their own way. It is they who set the tone for what the right appearance of justice is. This attitude, of course, increases the tensions between the wealthy and the poor. Just as class war issued in the existence of the democracy, it now ends it, as we will see in the next portrait.

THE TYRANNY

Tyranny follows upon democracy. In a democracy, the many now have the political authority. Thus, the many begin to chip away

Ch. 9 Portrait of Justice as a Useful Good

at the privilege of the rich, who are fewer in number. The rich, fearing to be despoiled utterly, begin to organize and then fight back. A civil war begins, the rich being successful at first because of their superior skills and great wealth. But along comes a talented but unscrupulous "Champion of the People." He is a former member of the upper class who has lost his position either because of his dissipated ways or because of being forced out by the competition of other rich people. He mobilizes the many so that they eventually win the conflict and despoil the rich.

But after the successful revolution, the leader now has to settle down to the difficult task of running a country whose economy, political institutions, and social fabric is in shambles. He begins to use the private army given to him by the people to prey on the people themselves. The people, then, end up worse off than they were before the civil war. For they are now under a shrewd master who has been well schooled in the arts of manipulation and of direct force. In this type of government, the political authority has been usurped by a figure whose sole purpose is to use the whole community for the maintenance of his ego. The goal of the ruler is not even the acquisition of some recognized human good like honor, wealth, pleasure or freedom, pursuits that would win the allegiance of some portion of the population. The goal is simply power for the ruler, and the means to attain this goal are both Sophisticated and unSophisticated forms of inducing fear.

THE TYRANT AS AN INDIVIDUAL

As an individual, the tyrant is the son of a typical parent in the age of the democracy. For a while, there is a struggle in the soul of this son between a certain decency and sheer profligacy. He goes the way of the profligate. Unlike many profligates, who destroy

Ch. 9 Portrait of Justice as a Useful Good

themselves by their excesses, he somehow survives physically. But he is beset by obsessions and addictions, which give him a crazy kind of energy. He is a Captain Ahab, whose goal to destroy Moby Dick was insane, but whose means were as sane as the most resourceful chess master.

He is no longer driven by the normal vices but is prisoner to sick cravings. Having shed blood in his many political adventures, he is like a wolf who, having tasted human flesh, cannot stop feeding himself. But he is also a smart wolf, having survived the many adventures that finished off other wolves of less resourcefulness.

As smart as he is, however, the tyrant is a slave to his sick passions. He really has no personal center within himself but is a bundle of contradictory impulses. And just as he is a slave to his own passions, so he enslaves the community under him. The political community itself, then, becomes a bundle of sick passions trampling upon any vestige of the human person.

SUMMARY

In his account of the career of justice pursued as a useful good, Plato has shown that the initial abandonment of reason to the rule of the appetites leads to the pursuit of utilitarian justice, then to the appearance of justice, and finally to the full horror of naked vice. This abandonment of reason means that human beings refuse to accept the objective order of things; namely, the intrinsic worth or structure of humanity.

Seduced by the short-term promises of using the Ring of Gyges, people are repelled by a Socrates and attracted to a Sophist. The young, who have little experience of life, are especially prone to this seduction. Thus, they consider people who can do anything they wish as the models for happiness. But Socrates forces the audience to look at life as

Ch. 9 Portrait of Justice as a Useful Good

it really happens. To help this focus, he almost seems to welcome the restriction not to appeal to any rewards or punishments in an afterlife. So, he plays out for the audience in words what actual living does for people in experience.

THE WINNER DECLARED

At the conclusion of his account of the tyrant (in Book Nine), there is little tension about who is the winner in this comparison between justice as an intrinsic good and justice as a useful good. It is clear that individuals and communities that opt for the former will be happy while those opting for the latter will be miserable. It is also clear that Socrates is a better human being than the tyrant, who is a logical extension of the Sophist. Though Socrates will be condemned to death for his views, he shows himself to be an impressive human being. Having tried all his life to respect the objective good, he lives by the truth that it is far worse to do rather than to suffer evil. Thus, Socrates has a human center which draws the respect of others like him.

In contrast to Socrates is the tyrant, who has the power to kill anybody he wishes and to avoid being killed by anybody. The tyrant has made as an absolute rule for himself that his own death is to be avoided at any cost. Therefore, he feels that it is far better to do rather than to suffer evil. In time, the tyrant runs out of all the tricks of appearances and must rely on naked force. Thus, the tyrant ends up alone, not as far as gathering a crowd is concerned, but as far as having any decent relationship with another human being. For the tyrant really has no personal center but is within a multitude of conflicting forces. Socrates describes this person as a creature, which, though it has the outward form of a human, has no reason at all. The spirited appetite of this creature is like a raging lion. The pleasure appetite is a many-headed,

Ch. 9 Portrait of Justice as a Useful Good

serpentine monster with open mouths ready to bite and devour anything within reach. This creature is human only in the sense that irrational animals could never develop into this state. Only humans with the power of choice could so frustrate the potential of their human nature they pervert their natural drives to become a menace both to themselves and to others.

According to Plato, then, there is such a thing as "the right way to live." The Sophist would reject this norm as being too rigid, too restrictive of human freedom. He would maintain that there are as many right ways to live as there are different people living. But Plato shows that people who are initially seduced by this view enter upon a path in which all options are destructive of the humanity of both self and others. Thus, the path that starts with the promise that there are many right ways to live ends up at the destination in which there is no right way to live.

THE MEDIEVAL CATHEDRAL

In concluding this section of the argument, we might compare the philosophical structure erected by Plato as similar to the Medieval Cathedral. The old builders aimed to construct an edifice whose size would amaze travelers seeing it from afar and provide great space for the worshippers within. It would require a high ceiling and a wide floor. The high ceiling in turn would demand tall walls to support it. And the wide floor would necessitate that the ceiling and roof span a great distance. The result would be that the weight of the ceiling and roof on the supporting walls would exert a thrust, farcing those walls outward. The higher the walls, the less capable they would be of resisting the outward thrust.

Something would have to be done to keep the high walls up if the Cathedral were to be built. The builders had to do more than to dig deep foundations to support the main

Ch. 9 Portrait of Justice as a Useful Good

structure. While deep foundations would support the great weight of the walls, they would not enable the walls to withstand the outward thrust of the roof. The builders finally solved the problem: they united their soaring dreams with the demands of the practical by inventing the flying buttress. These were columns of stone, which function like the rows of two-by-fours which builders place against the sagging walls of a house. The foundations of these columns rest many yards outside of the exterior walls. The columns themselves lean over into the wall. And their tops terminate at points along the walls just below the ceiling and the roof. Thus, they met the thrust of the walls being pushed out with their own thrust pushing back. All along the outside walls, then, the flying buttresses are anchored so that, while initially conceived as exterior supports to the main structure, they became a dramatic and characteristic part of it.

PLATO'S STRUCTURE

Plato has built a definition of the nature of justice by first digging deep into human experience to find the foundation, which is the nature of man himself. Upon this nature in both its communal and individual aspects he has placed the virtue of justice as an intrinsic good which, as we saw, is equivalent to wisdom, courage, and moderation perfecting or completing the nature of man. The more cynical, however, reject these virtues because they seem too lofty to be practical in this earth of ours. To meet this possible rejection, Plato then employs the very cynicism of the cynics to prove his point. As if using them like flying buttresses, Plato allows them to state to the fullest their opposing position so that the reader can see clearly the sheer opposition between them. The result, I believe, is a magnificent philosophical structure, which shows without a shadow of a doubt that there is such a thing

Ch. 9 Portrait of Justice as a Useful Good

as the right way to live. There is such a thing as justice. Knowing this in a philosophical way equips people like Glaucon with a clear standard, which they can use to judge and evaluate what goes on in the City of Man. Now, they know not only that justice as intrinsic is a good thing; they know why it is good.

With this insight, they then know how to defend intellectually the position that the pursuit of virtue is not merely a luxury for the refined, or a duty for the religious. It is an absolute necessity for human beings if they wish to avoid making their communal and individual lives a hell on earth.

A LOOK AHEAD

This is all one needs to know in order to be logically satisfied that justice is an intrinsic good. However, one can know all there is to know about a particular structure in front of them and yet not really understand it. To understand it, one must know its purpose, which is the ultimate reason why the structure has the shape it has. One does not really understand a Medieval Cathedral who does not know that it was built for the glory of God.

So, too, one does not fully understand the argument defining the nature of justice unless one knows the ultimate purpose of justice. The more immediate purpose of justice, as we have repeatedly said, is man's attainment of happiness. But why is it that man exists? Why is his nature the way it is? Why should his goal be happiness? The answer to all these questions lies in examining the place that God holds in Plato's scheme of things. This will be our concern for the next chapter.

CHAPTER TEN

DIVINE CAUSES

INTRODUCTION

So far, we have not paid any attention to the religious or the divine element in Plato's account of justice. Although we (like Plato) started off our consideration of justice by examining the experience of an old man who has become more religious with the passage of time, we (also like Plato) have left out of our argument about justice the very considerations that motivated the old man to live the way he did. These considerations were his fear of death, his belief in the gods, his desire for repentance, and his conviction that there was indeed an afterlife in which he would be rewarded or punished for his deeds. Why has Plato omitted up to this point such important factors in the discussion of justice? The reason is that in Chapter Six, Glaucon forbade Socrates to bring into the argument any consideration of an afterlife. That condition was accepted to clear away any obstacles that would impede the understanding that justice is an intrinsic good and, therefore, something that should be pursued for its own sake. There is a danger that if one relies totally upon arguments based upon reward and punishment in the afterlife as the only motive for being just, one might obscure the truth that justice is a good thing even *before* one dies. One might even be in danger of giving others the impression that being just is really a very dull experience we endure only because we are afraid of going to hell. This approach violates the truth that justice, being a good in itself, is very much a

Ch. 10 Divine Causes

good for this life as well as the next. Therefore, as I have said above, we have so far concentrated our attention on showing that justice is indeed a good by drawing upon the evidence supplied by this life only.

Yet the fact remains that Plato was also a religious man who holds for the existence of the gods and of an afterlife with rewards and punishments. It is also a fact that he approves of the religious experience of Cephalus, the old man. That is why Plato, after having finished his argument in Book Nine about justice being an intrinsic good, concludes his whole work in Book Ten with an account of the Myth of Er,[24] a story of how souls are judged by the gods in the afterlife. Confident that he has shown the intrinsic nature of justice, he now fills out the whole picture so the reader can place justice in its proper context.

---

[24] See section 614b.

Yet even before this, particularly in Books Six and Seven, Plato discusses such matters as the Ideal Forms and The Good, all of them being non-material realities. In Book Three,[25] he insists that the very first thing a community must do in educating the young is to teach them to have a much higher notion of the gods than the poets, even the great ones like Homer, seem to have. Plato then has made no secret of his religious belief in the gods and his philosophical conviction that there is an immaterial realm vastly more important than this material one.

THE RELIGIOUS AND SPIRITUAL CONTEXT

Now is the time to consider the religious and spiritual context in which justice, as an intrinsic good is set. Our intent to consider this context is driven mainly by a

---

[25] See section 377b.

Ch. 10 Divine Causes

philosophical reason or, to put it another way, by a desire for really understanding the nature of justice considered either as an intrinsic or as a useful good. We already have some insight into these notions because we have judged them using happiness as the objective standard. In other words, we have taken the final cause of human actions, their goal or purpose and explained the notion of justice in terms of it. In short, we have made the notion of justice intelligible by explaining it in the light of its final cause, happiness. The explanation is that only the pursuit of justice as an intrinsic good leads to happiness.

Now, it is time to take the whole universe in which human beings have a place and ask whether it too has a cause. In other words, we will be asking whether there is a Divine Realm. The particular point of this question will not be to launch upon a discussion of metaphysics directly, but to show that, if there is Divine Realm, then the proper notion of justice must be as an intrinsic good. On the other hand, if there is no Divine Realm, the proper notion of justice could easily seem to be as a useful good.

IF THERE IS A GOD

Plato holds that the gods exist.[26] They are purely spiritual in nature and therefore immortal, good, wise, and powerful. They are superior to man and indeed are the makers and rulers of the world. Here, we have a two-tiered universe; the Immortals are above (as causes) and the Mortals are below (as effects).

Holding that man lives in a two-tiered universe fundamentally determines the view that a thinker takes of morality or justice. Let us see why. If the nature of man is designed by the gods, then man is expected to act according to this design. Man is not his own

---

[26] For a rather complete discussion of the gods by Plato, see his *The Laws*, Book X.

Ch. 10 Divine Causes

master. The gods are. Thus, he is under obligation, under obedience, under duty.

If his actions perfect or complete this design, then he has fulfilled his nature and will be happy both in this life and in the next. This is not simply because of the will of the gods, as if they could change it at a mere whim. It is because man has his design from the gods as pottery will have its design from the potter. The gods can no more change the rules for the workings of that design than the potter can change the shape of a pot that has been fired.

If, on the other hand, man's actions mar or deface his own design, then he has frustrated his nature and will be miserable both in this life and the next. Consequently, the virtues are of absolute importance in this scheme of things. They perfect the nature of man so that he can achieve both individual and communal harmony. Therefore, the virtues are not mere instruments or tools to be used by man as he sees fit. They are qualities of great worth or value in themselves.

Wisdom, for example, perfects reason, man's highest faculty, so that it can exercise its highest function. What is that? To contemplate the highest realities, the gods. On this view, the next best thing to actually being a god is to be able to behold one. A lesser, but also an important, function of reason is to rule the appetites so that man will be courageous and temperate. If he does not rule his appetites, he will never be able to be a contemplative, to be a lover of the truth for its own sake.

FURTHER CONSEQUENCES

One like Socrates, who holds to the reality of a two-tiered universe, will consider that it would be far worse for him to do evil than to suffer it, far worse to murder or rape than to be murdered or raped. For in doing evil, for which he is responsible, he ruins his own

Ch. 10 Divine Causes

soul, which is the immortal part of his nature designed by the gods, and so displeases the gods. On the contrary, in suffering evil for the right reason, even at the loss of his life, he enhances his own soul and pleases the gods. In standing up for the truth at the risk of his life, he honors the gods. In brief, if the only choice he has is between the practice of virtue and the saving of his own life, the good man picks virtue and surrenders his life.

OBJECTIVE

It goes without saying that the norms or standards of this way of life are objective—they are the same for all human beings without exception. They are timeless—they perfect man's nature, which remains the same throughout the ages. The nature neither of the gods nor of man will change. They are also absolute—there are deeds which no human being may do under any circumstance, deeds like murdering or cheating. No king or government or leader may murder even one innocent person for any reason whatsoever, even for the reason supposedly of the survival of the leaders and the whole State. Only the gods are masters of life and death. They, ultimately, are the Rulers of the Human City. Therefore, this prohibition does not change with the evolution of different cultures, histories, epochs. For what difference can these changes make to the gods?

THE KEYSTONE

Let us however remove the keystone of the moral structure above and then see what happens. Let us say that there are no gods. Then man lives in a one-tiered universe in which he is the master and ruler. For intelligence takes priority over mere matter, which may be bigger by light years. Thus, man is subject to no master other than himself. It is he who will put the design into reality. It is he who will determine what should be done or not done.

Hence, everything, not justice alone, is a tool or instrument to be used by such a creature as a means to an end of his choosing. The first tool will be his own reason. No longer will its chief function be the contemplation of what is above it to attain immutable truth. Its chief function will be to implement what his will or appetites desire. It will be creative, active, and aggressive in producing truth, not contemplating it.

A RELATIVE SCHEME

It goes without saying that such a scheme of morality (if one may call it that) is entirely relative. There is no standard outside of Man according to which deeds are right or wrong. Instead, Man himself sets his own standard according to his own wishes. This moral code then is relative. It is wildly relative when one considers that there is no such thing as Man but that there are only individual human beings. If Man, as such, is a god, then each human being is also a god. And here we have the condition laid out by the Sophist in which each human being strives to be absolutely free.

This moral code is also time bound. If it changes with the desires of each individual agent, it also changes with the times. It is also historically conditioned. For, though the theory is that all men are god-like, some are a lot more god-like than others. Thus, the superior classes lay down what is right and just, the other accepting or rejecting it as best they can.

GREATEST EVIL

In this scheme of things, it will be far worse to suffer evil rather than to do it, to endure murder or rape rather than to murder or rape. For one's own life is the only thing in the universe of absolute value. Thus, to lose or to mar it is the ultimate evil. While one may regret doing evil to another, one has even more regret for suffering evil oneself. For enduring evil is to be the Victim while doing it is to be the Aggressor. One may not like being either. But one must admit that being an Aggressor seems to be a lot more godlike than being a helpless Victim.

INTIMATE CONNECTION

We see then that there is an intimate connection between holding for the notion of justice as an intrinsic good and holding for the existence of Divine Realm. We see that there is also a solid connection between holding for justice as a useful good and holding for Atheism. A knowledge of the basic reasons behind positions makes them far more intelligible than an examination, even if thorough, of the positions themselves. That is why we have concluded our treatment of justice by a consideration of the highest causes.

AS A WAY OF CONCLUDING

As a way of concluding this examination of Plato's argument in *The Republic*, let us consider his great Parable of the Cave[27] in Book Seven. For that parable summarizes all of the main themes of this inquiry in a most graphic way. The story opens with a great number of people watching what might be called a motion picture located in a large cave deep down in the earth. The audience, however, considers the pictures to be realities. This is not surprising since they are chained to their seats and unable to turn away from the scenes depicted in front of them. Moreover, they are delighted with these pictures.

---

[27] See section 514.

Ch. 10 Divine Causes

At a certain point, one of the members of the audience, somehow freed of his fetters, turns around and sees that the pictures that everyone has been taking for reality are not reality. He tries to tell the others about his discovery but is shouted down as a nuisance. The divine force that has liberated him from his chains also drags him kicking and screaming up the long incline leading from the depths to the mouth of the cave. When he reaches the top, he is blinded by the sunlight and cannot see the realities around him—animals, people, fields, and trees. But as he gets used to the light, he begins to understand what is real. He is so happy to be in the upper world that he has no desire to go back into the cave to instruct his fellows about what is real. He knows he will not be welcome. Nevertheless, he does go back down. His eyes, used to the sun, have a hard time getting used to the shadows and the darkness. His blindness is interpreted as stupidity and slowness; he cannot see what his fellows consider to be real. The story ends there with our hero trying to tell his fellows about what is shadow and what is reality.

INTERPRETATION

The parable represents the two-tiered universe. On the lower level is the human race, engrossed in the pursuit of power, riches, and pleasure, all the things that pander to man's appetites undirected by reason. People consider these things to be the only realities, non-material things being the same as nothing at all. Plato, however, considers them as mere images or shadows. What is fully real is the reality above.

The man, released from his chains, is someone like Socrates, who is saved by divine dispensation from accepting the shadows of the world as reality. He tries to tell the people that it is they who live in unreality, not people like him. He is then urged along the difficult path of philosophy until he arrives at a peak and sees all things in the light cast by The Good. Just as the earthly sun by its heat and light is both the cause of the things in this world and the reason why our eyes can see them, so there is the immaterial form called The Good, which, by the light it casts upon the human mind, enables the philosopher to see what is really real. The true definition of justice would be an example of one of these Forms or Ideas.[28]

IS THE GOOD A GOD?

Is The Good a god or is it a Form even superior to the gods?[29] What are the other forms to which The Good is related? These are interesting questions over which scholars still debate. But there is no need to concern ourselves with these matters here. What does

---

[28] See section 493e.

[29] A good book to read on these questions is Etienne Gilson's *God and Philosophy*, Yale University Press, 1941.

concern us is the place the Forms or Ideas have in Plato's philosophy. They stand for the natures or essences which the material things of this world share in some way. That is why when any inquirer strives to penetrate to the definition of a thing, he is striving for a more complete idea of the form which the individual thing shares. Are these pure Forms or Ideas immaterial realities existing in themselves and apart from the material things that participate in them?[30] This is what Plato seems to maintain and this seems to be the way he speaks of them in many passages in *The Republic.* But there is no need at this point for us to concern ourselves about that matter. What is our concern is the way Plato insists that the question of the definition of virtue is a matter that can be decided by

---

[30] I accept this view on the condition that these pure Forms or Ideas are simply ideas in the mind of God. That is the solution of the medieval theologians, who make the Ideas of Plato the Divine Ideas of the One God.

reason. This question we have asked ourselves; and to answer it we have embarked upon a long inquiry into the definition of justice. Have we arrived at the truth of the matter? I say that we have. But it is up to each reader to answer that question for himself.

THE END OF OUR INQUIRY

We have come to the end of our inquiry. We started with the experience of a religious person like the old man Cephalus and translated it into the precise form of a philosophical explanation. It only remains for us to review what we have done as far as it relates to the Catholic tradition of the natural law.

AFTERWORD

Perhaps the best way for me to begin showing the connection between our inquiry and the Catholic tradition of natural law is to speak from my own experience, even at the risk of repeating some of the things I have said in the Introduction. My confidence had been shaken in the Catholic Tradition I had been raised in. I was like Glaucon, having had my ears filled with all kinds of argument that chipped away at my moral sense of things. I had never seriously questioned the teaching that there are moral standards, which are absolute, objective, universal, and true. But many Catholic moral theologians were questioning it all around me. They spoke of a "new understanding" of morality that was not rigid but adapted to circumstances, that was not based upon "impersonal abstractions" but upon "compassion" for everyone in the human condition. They spoke of a newer and richer understanding of the natural law. I was not absolutely against this type of talk; the Catholic traditional teaching is hard enough to have inspired me with some desire to soften it, both for myself and for others. But I was not entirely for it either—it seemed to throw the whole tradition aside, surely a serious thing for a Catholic like myself to contemplate.

The moral thinking of my students didn't so much confuse as depress me. They were moral relativists without even knowing it. When the notion was explained to them, they readily admitted to it as if it were the most natural thing in the world. They were Catholic students with Catholic training but did not seem to feel any great contradiction between being both Catholics and moral

Afterword

relativists. Even when they decided to live according to a strong moral code, they figured that it was their choice and others had the right to make another choice if they saw fit. In short, it seemed that the World had done a very thorough job of educating them into being "tolerant," "open minded," "compassionate," and "freedom loving" young men and women.

At a certain point, I got sick of weighing arguments pro and con, especially arguments that brought in theology and the Church. I just had to think of the word "Church" and a thousand-person chorus started rioting in my head, each member shouting out his own view. Besides, the Church made me feel guilty, always calling me and everyone else a sinner. I didn't mind it calling others sinners—they were! But I was a lot more sensitive about putting myself in that category. Feeling guilty about being branded a sinner is not the best way to face the question of moral absolutes.

The Right Way to Live

In this state of mind, I resolved to use *The Republic* to teach philosophical ethics. My intention was to sit back and simply watch Socrates in action as I went through the book with my students. The fact that he was a pagan and had lived a long time ago were all assets as far as I was concerned. There was no danger that he would scare me with the words "The Catholic Church says..." At the end, I was deeply impressed with the notion that the possession of virtue is not a luxury for the individual and society. It is an absolute necessity that rulers rule for the sake of the community and not for themselves and that reason controls appetite. I was surprised to discover that the whole matter is really that simple.

The careful and even tedious way in which Plato goes about establishing this truth adds to the effect. He lays out the steps of the argument like a builder carefully putting blocks of stone together to build some monument. The starting point is made clear.

Afterword

The logical steps leading from it are connected. And the conclusion they lead to is finally inevitable. He was using the method of Science, which the Greeks, who invented it all, applied to moral matters with even greater eagerness than they applied it to mathematical or physical questions. Aristotle called this application Ethics or Political philosophy and ranked that study the very highest of all the practical sciences.

Having finally seen that the question about the reality of moral absolutes is not really that complicated intellectually, I began to look upon the Church with renewed respect. For many of the objections that the outside world and many of her inside intellectuals made against the moral tradition of the Church could just as well have been made against Plato. Plato held for human nature being a constant throughout time—modern intellectuals don't, but the Church does. The Greek philosopher held for certain moral standards that did not change as cultures changed, that did not evolve, as perhaps some animal might—modern intellectuals don't, but the Church does. He held that Reason could know with certitude the validity of certain broad truths about the right way to live—modern intellectuals don't, but the Church does. There was no doubt in my mind that Plato was right. And there was no doubt that the Church, through her Magisterium, was the only institution which held consistently, in the past and in the present, for the objective nature of moral norms, a stand that has made her despised by many today.

I felt like a sheep with horns all bent and broken, who finally began to hone in on the Shepherd's voice amidst all the competing noises. Plato had tuned up my ears. And now I could hear the right voice. It was that of Christ, of the Church. For the Church is the Body of Christ. In hearing the right voice, I also began to get a line on those other voices. They were really articulating the objections

Afterword

against morality that an Atheist might and not really building upon the Tradition at all. Did not Nietzsche, who proclaimed that God is dead, oppose all the positions of Plato? And did not Nietzsche claim that Christianity was simply a watered-down version of Platonism? How then could the new breed of Catholic intellectuals derive any positive inspiration from the work of that man and neglect the work of someone like St. Thomas, who fashioned the classical expression of the natural law teaching?

Having tuned into the key questions put by Plato, I began to be educated by events over the years to the fact that there was and is a huge battle going on between the Church and the modern world over the fate of man. The world seems to have been successful in convincing large numbers that there is no such thing as a human nature, which is the same for every human being that ever lived. Further, great numbers do not think of the family as a natural institution but simply as one human constant alongside of other possible arrangements: The result seems to be that the natural cannot hold its own against the attacks of society. Men seem to have cultivated a bent for being as unnatural as possible. Alone of all institutions is the Church holding for the reality of human nature, of the family as a natural institution.

It seems as if the supernatural is needed not just to get human beings into heaven, but also to save the natural here on this earth. In my younger days, I would have thought that the natural could take care of itself. When I heard the expression "Grace builds upon Nature," I thought of Nature sitting there and Grace being put on top of it. But time has taught me that Nature isn't just sitting there alone waiting for Grace to come. Rather, it is still there only because Grace has all along been nurturing and protecting it. The Church, of course, bears this Grace, calling human beings to it as a Mother Hen calls its chicks. One can love a Church like that!

Afterword

One of the ways the Church saves human nature is to save its reason so that, when it thinks, it understands more and not less of reality. And one of the ways it saves reason is by instructing those who have time for books in the tradition of the natural law. Utilizing the insight of St. Thomas, the Church places the entire design for man in the mind of God, calling it the Eternal Law. When God creates man, He makes man so that his reason has the power to see in a basic and general way what he should or should not do. Another and perhaps more graphic way of putting it is to say that the natural norms of the law are placed within the heart of man. If men follow their reason or their hearts (call it conscience), they will develop the virtues, which will enable them to follow it even more faithfully. If men do not follow their consciences, they develop the vices, which so pervert their natures that they cannot endure the sight, feel, touch, or smell of the natural.

Again, one can indeed love a Church that teaches like that. But if this Church were merely a human institution, one would fear for its survival today. Socrates and Plato feared for the survival of Athens. All that Plato could do was write his book, many years after Athens fell. Plato thought long and hard about what the Human City needed. It needed a Philosopher King.[31] He also knew enough about life to realize that it was most unlikely that such a figure would ever come. Yet he hoped. And there came such a figure who was more than a philosopher and more than a king. It was God who became a baby and set up a Church, which was also his body.

So, the battle continues between Socrates and Thrasymachus, Plato and the Sophist. Except in this new script, God himself is on the side of justice considered as an intrinsic good. And He will not lose this argument, any

---

[31] See section 473d.

Afterword

more than Socrates lost his. Except He, unlike Socrates, will build more than theories.

INDEX

-A-

absolutes
  moral, vii, 134, 271, 273
Adeimantus, 156-157
afterlife, 51, 157, 214, 241, 250-251
analogy, 87-88
  for community, 167
appearance, 16, 22, 150-152, 164, 200, 216, 223-224, 231, 234, 236, 240, 242
appetite
  pleasure, 211-213, 242
  spirited, 211-213, 242
appetites, 203, 207-208, 210, 218, 226, 229, 231, 233, 240, 256, 259, 264, 272
arts
  technical, 17, 31, 37-38, 75, 87, 196

atheism, 54, 261

Athens, viii, x, 42-44, 47-48, 62-63, 85, 278

-C-

cathedral, 244, 248

cause
 divine, 249
 final, 253

Cephalus, 47, 50, 52, 53, 57, 68, 102, 107, 192, 217, 251, 267
 religion of, 52, 251

Christ, vi, viii, 274

Church, ii-x, 13-15, 112, 271-278

community
 conflictual, 166-171, 186, 188
 cooperative, 166-167, 174-178, 186-188, 191-195, 201-202
 organic, 166, 173, 175, 177-178, 181, 183, 188, 191, 194-195, 197, 199

compromise, 143

conscience, iii, ix, x, 37, 39, 54, 56, 58, 78, 83-84, 136, 152, 277

counter-example, 65
courage, 48, 191, 194, 201-203, 205, 213, 217, 231, 246, 256

-D-

definition
  process of, 17-18, 27-28, 33, 38-39, 65, 91, 123, 219
democracy, 93, 144, 236, 238
design, 31, 178, 254-255, 277
division of the soul
  tripartite, 206

-E-

End (also goal), 24, 26, 31, 70, 75, 97-98, 126-130, 132, 137, 141, 145, 152, 154, 169, 175, 177, 196, 197, 204-205, 228, 233, 236, 238, 239, 248, 253
ethics
  philosophical, i, v, 272
  sexual, vii, 184-185

evil
   goal, 75
   greatest, 260-261
   intrinsic, 14
   man, 159
   morally, 126-128, 141
   necessary, 121-122, 143
   purpose, 71, 75
experience
   ordinary, 27, 33, 35, 137, 204, 211, 217
   religious, 107, 251

-F-

faith, I, iii, iv, v, x, 134
   and reason, v, xi, 14, 140
family, 181-185, 188, 275-276
flying buttress, 245-246
form
   literary, 45
foundation, 33, 39, 41, 59, 107, 117, 181, 192, 244-246

Afterword

-G-

Glaucon, 110-112, 114-115, 118-119, 123-124, 130-131, 135-136, 140-142, 149, 156, 163-165, 192, 214, 217-222, 247, 250, 269
goal. See end.
good
  intrinsic, 114, 122, 126, 130, 152, 158-159, 167, 188, 191-192, 206, 214, 221, 241, 246-247, 250-253, 261, 278
  three types of, 119
Gyges, 145-148, 153, 170, 201, 222, 240

-H-

happiness, 129, 132-133, 136-138, 141-142, 177, 192, 194-196, 199, 217, 223, 240, 248, 253
heart, ix, x, 56, 85, 88, 111, 147, 158-159, 196, 209, 211, 216, 277
honor, 73, 112, 130, 148, 156, 197, 212, 224, 227-229, 231-233, 236, 238, 257

-I-

ideal standard, 224-225
immutability, 106
inquiry,
   art of, 78
   communal, 66, 82, 90, 130
   intellectual, 18-19, 78
   philosophical, 53, 222
   starting point, 133, 138, 272
irony, 89

-J-

Job, 155-156
Judeo-Christian, 184
justice
   as an art, 70, 75-76, 93
   as an intrinsic good, 114, 122, 126, 130, 152, 158-159, 167, 188, 191-192, 206, 214, 221, 241, 246-247, 250-253, 261, 278

definition of, 18, 57, 75, 77, 81, 84, 92, 101-102, 120, 132, 191-192, 265, 267

-K-

keystone, 258

-L-

law
  natural, iii, v, vii, 15, 54, 56-57, 78, 83, 100, 103, 140, 267, 269-270, 275, 277
Laws, the, 254

-M-

Magisterium, ii-iii, 274
morality
  popular, 61, 72-74, 79, 144
  relativism, 13-15, 17, 26, 58
  sexual, 179, 181, 188
  traditional, 102, 186

-O-

oligarchy, 232

-P-

parable
  of the Cave, 262
philosopher King, 278
Plato
  background, 42
Polemarchus, 62-63, 65, 68, 70-77, 81-84, 96, 146
political science
  modern, 161, 176, 199

-R-

reason
  related to emotions, 207-209
Republic, The
  date of composition, 44

Afterword

-S-

Socrates
  background, 43, 48
St. Thomas, v, vi, 140, 275, 277
standard, 25, 128, 132, 137, 192, 253

-T-

Thrasymachus, 63, 81-102, 109-114, 145, 278
timelessness, 106
timocracy, 227, 232
tyranny, 183, 236

-U-

unchanging, viii, 134
universe
  one-tiered, 258
  two-tiered, 254, 256, 264

-V-

virtue
- Courage. See courage.
- definition of, 33, 266
- fortitude, 231-232
- justice. See justice.
- Moderation, 191, 194, 203, 217, 246
- necessary to the rulers, 195
- prudence, 196-197
- temperance, 203-204, 213
- wisdom, 191, 194, 196, 198, 213, 228, 246, 256

About the Author

As a professor of philosophy for many decades, Richard Geraghty has been rated the most popular of teachers because of his gift not only for simplifying difficult concepts, but also for expounding them with brilliance and humor.

Until his death in 2017, Richard served as a professor of philosophy at St. Joseph's House of Studies, the college-level facility of the Franciscan Missionaries of the Eternal Word at EWTN.

Over the course of his career, Richard taught philosophy at the University of Dayton, Providence College, St. John's College Seminary, and Holy Apostles College & Seminary.

His book *A Companion to Reading Newman's Grammar of Assent* was published posthumously by En Route Books & Media in 2017.

www.ingramcontent.com/pod-product-compliance
Lightning Source LLC
Chambersburg PA
CBHW071131160426
43196CB00011B/1855